Havasupai Legends

Havasupai Legends

Religion and Mythology of the
Havasupai Indians of the
Grand Canyon

Carma Lee Smithson and
Robert C. Euler

University of Utah Press
Salt Lake City

Originally published as University of Utah Anthropological Papers no. 68,
April 1964, with the title *Havasupai Religion and Mythology*

∞ Printed on acid-free paper
Photographs courtesy of Robert C. Euler

LIBRARY OF CONGRESS CATALOGING-IN-PUBLICATION DATA

Smithson, Carma Lee.
    [Havasupai religion and mythology]
    Havasupai legends : religion and mythology of the Havasupai Indians
of the Grand Canyon / Carma Lee Smithson and Robert C. Euler.
       p.   cm.
    Originally published: Havasupai religion and mythology. Salt Lake
City : University of Utah Press, 1964, in series: University of Utah anthropological papers ; no. 68.
    Includes bibliographical references.
    ISBN 0-87480-446-9 (paperback : acid-free paper)
    1. Havasupai Indians—Legends.   2. Havasupai Indians—Religion
and mythology.   I. Title.
E99.H3S56   1994
398.2'089975—dc20
                                 93-41857

Contents

Preface

The Havasupai Indians have lived in the depths of western Grand Canyon and surrounding uplands of the South Rim for almost seven hundred years. Their aboriginal territory, before it was usurped by Anglo-Americans, consisted of more than seven million acres, extending from the Grand Canyon on the north, south to present-day Interstate Highway 40, east to the Hopi villages, and west to the Havasupai's neighbors and linguistic relatives, the Hualapai near Peach Springs, Arizona.

In this vast territory that ranged from more than seven thousand feet above sea level in the uplands to eighteen hundred feet at the Colorado River in Grand Canyon they hunted, farmed at well-watered spots, and gathered wild food over the greatest altitude range of any Indians in the southwestern United States. Deer and desert bighorn sheep lived in the many canyons tributary to the South Rim of Grand Canyon. Rabbits and other smaller game could be found everywhere. Edible wild plants, especially the *Agave* or century plant, were abundant and varied throughout their territory, and the farms of corn, beans, and squash were extensive in their summer home in the bottom of Havasu Canyon. There they lived in brush and mud-covered huts; in the winter, on the plateau above, rock shelters and brush wickiups sufficed.

Prior to A.D. 1300, when archaeologists first have a record of them in this broad country, the region was occupied by another, unrelated group of prehistoric Indians, the Cohonina. These Indians, known only from archaeological excavations, abandoned the area about A.D. 1150, probably because of severe drought. For almost 150 years, the region was uninhabited until the Havasupai and the Hualapai—the Pai—moved eastward from the lower Colorado River.

The sociopolitical organization of the Havasupai was relatively simple, with families and extended families loosely organized in a patrilineal fashion. There were, indeed, nominal bands composed of several families, members of which followed a respected headman to the plateau on one side of Havasu Canyon or the other during the fall and winter exodus from the Canyon. Beyond that, there was no formal political structure.

Medicine men or shamans were of great importance, however. Respected and feared because of their abilities to cure illnesses and to control the weather, these shamans were thought to receive supernatural powers from spirit beings who came to them in visions or dreams. Since the Havasupai possessed no great scientific knowledge, they, like most nonliterate peoples around the world, believed in these supernatural powers and this belief provided them religious sustenance and at least a modicum of health.

When the first European, Father Francisco Garces, visited them in their canyon homeland in 1776, the Havasupai still carried on most of their aboriginal life. From their Hopi friends to the east they had obtained a few European goods, but aside from occasional raids by the Yavapai from the south near present-day Prescott, and to a lesser extent from Paiutes who lived across the Grand Canyon to the north, there were few interruptions to the native life of the Havasupai. In addition to their Hopi trading partners, the Havasupai had friendly relations with the Hualapai, Mojave, and the Halchidoma, all speakers of Yuman dialects. Navajos were not then in direct contact with the Havasupai.

For at least a half century following Garces's visit in 1776 the Havasupai attracted little attention from Europeans. During the period of Mexican sovereignty, aside from a few raids by Mexican slave hunters, life changed little. But in 1848, after the treaty of Guadalupe Hidalgo, Pai territory become part of the United States. Within a decade American emigrants convoyed wagon trains across northern Arizona. Skirmishes with the Mojave occurred as these emigrants attempted to cross the Colorado River to California. By the 1860s, these Anglo newcomers had begun to harass the Hualapai. From 1866 to 1869 the Hualapai battled almost continuously with United States troops, to protect their territory and their way of life from the Anglo-American intruders. Yet the Havasupai, out of the main route of travel, were relatively untouched by this turmoil, even though some of them joined a Hualapai tribal-scale force engaging the U.S. Army.

Beginning in the late 1860s and increasingly through the next two decades, miners and prospectors sought mineral wealth in the territory of the defeated Pai, particularly in Havasu Canyon. The federal government, acquiescing to these prospectors, finally set aside a 518-acre reservation for the Havasupai in 1882. This land was restricted to their farms and their summer village thus freeing for exploitation the mineral zones as well as all of native Havasupai territory elsewhere in Grand Canyon and on the plateau above. By such actions United States officials dealt a death-blow to sustainable Havasupai economic life, forcing them into nearly abject poverty.

In 1893 President Benjamin Harrison proclaimed Grand Canyon a forest preserve. Later, without regard to aboriginal land rights, Grand Canyon was set aside as a National Monument and game preserve. Havasupai were virtually imprisoned in their tiny Canyon reservation.

In the 1890s another facet of industrial civilization impinged directly upon the daily lives of the increasingly beleaguered Havasupai. Anglo schoolteachers came to Havasu Canyon to teach the Indian children Christianity, English reading and writing, and government farmers arrived to teach the Havasupai techniques they had already mastered centuries before.

Havasupais were encouraged to cease their "heathen" practice of cremating the dead and to curtail the "idolatrous ways" of native shamans; the Bureau of Indian Affairs began to provide the rudiments of "modern medicine." Still the Havasupai attempted to carry on what religious beliefs they had left. Cremation of the dead and their possessions were intended to keep the *kwidjati* or ghosts from returning to upset the living. Havasupai religious practitioners also increased their efforts to cure the sick. However, diseases such as tuberculosis and syphilis plagued these people, now dominated by Anglo-Americans who brought these diseases to the Canyon. Practitioners made prayers to certain natural landmarks thought to be the home of spirits who were sometimes dangerous and sometimes beneficial in that they were thought to bring rain to this arid land.

In a desperate move to regain their native way of life, the

Havasupai and Hualapai adopted a nativistic movement from the Paiute in 1889, the Ghost Dance. The Ghost Dance, it was thought, would remove all white people, bring back the dwindling game, and allow a return to the old lifeways. They continued this dance for several years until, at last, they realized their efforts had failed.

Missionaries made continuing but sporadic efforts to convert the Havasupai to Christianity, although the Indians escaped the full brunt of missionary activity until 1948 when a quonset hut was helicoptered to their canyon village to serve the Episcopal church. Later, in 1956, a Baptist couple took over the building, but their efforts soon lapsed.

Yet native religious practices continued to wane. The last Havasupai shaman died in the early 1960s. Some mourning ceremonies, borrowed from the Mojave, were sung at funerals but these, too, were attenuated offerings. A harvest festival, known as the Peach Festival, continues, but this is now primarily a social affair.

At this writing, especially with the passage of the federal American Indian Religious Freedom Act, some Havasupai have once again become interested in their ancient practices. They have refused to reveal to National Park Service officials the locations of religious sites in Grand Canyon, having learned that the result is unauthorized visits or vandalism.

During the 1980s proposals to develop a small uranium mine south of Grand Canyon and many miles from the Havasupai Reservation came to the attention of the Havasupai Tribal Council. Fearing the possible effects such a mine might have on their water supply, they enlisted the aid of a tribal attorney to protest mine development. Somehow, during the course of legal testimony, the Havasupai began to assert religious significance for the mine site. Through their attorney they claimed in a case heard before the U.S. District Court, District of Arizona, that the mining site was "the Abdomen of the Mother of all Havasupai." This statement was greatly elaborated upon by the attorney discussing other matters of alleged religious practices.

In fact, no Havasupai had known about or visited the proposed mining site prior to this claim; no such claim was in evidence in any of the Havasupai anthropological or historical literature nor when Carma Lee Smithson and I interviewed Havasupai about religion. During my extensive fieldwork over the area with knowledgeable Havasupai guides, in preparation for the Havasupai land claim before the U.S. Indian Claims Commission, this was never mentioned. I note this because the assertion is now a matter of public record and persons interested in Havasupai religion may take it at face value.

About This Book

When Carma Lee Smithson and I conducted fieldwork on Havasupai religion and mythology, our respondents were most forthcoming; there was never an air of secretiveness or fabrication. We both had excellent rapport with tribal members and they understood that we were attempting to record for posterity what religious beliefs remained. Smithson's earlier monograph, *Havasupai Woman*, was well received and had the approval of the tribe.

Before her field investigations of Havasupai religion were complete, Smithson was diagnosed with lymphosarcoma and finally succumbed in 1961. The unpublished notes upon which this book is based came into my hands after her untimely death, at her initial request and through the courtesy of Jesse D. Jennings. When she first learned of her incurable illness, Smithson and I discussed the matter. This was at a time when I was working independently on other aspects of Havasupai culture but with essentially the same persons. We remain in her debt for concerning herself with the ultimate disposition of her notes during such a trying period of her life, and in that of Jennings for arranging for the editing and publication of the material. I should like, also, to express my appreciation to the University of Utah Research Fund for permitting me to utilize the unexpended balance of the grant in preparation of this monograph. I also wish to thank those unnamed Havasupai people who patiently helped me recheck portions of the notes and to add to them in the summer of 1962. Their cooperation was due in large measure to the rapport that Smithson had earlier established.

That the data are not full is a factor of several matters beyond the control of the authors. Smithson worked with last elderly Havasupai shaman who, in his advance years, had limitations of recall. He died prior to my 1962 visit, and lay informants had less knowledge of the more esoteric practices.

My contribution, then, in addition to brief fieldwork, was to clarify portions of the notes and put them into a more readable style and format, as well as to add comparative data. Direct statements are indicated as quotations.

In publishing these notes on religion and mythology, I feel that we are not only adding something to the data of Southwestern anthropology and providing information of benefit to present members of the tribe, but we are also paying respect to Carma Lee Smithson's dedication.

ROBERT C. EULER
1993

Religion

The Havasupai believed that the world was flat and that the sky was a dome that came to meet the earth all around the edges. The earth, high in the middle and sloping away to the edges, was small, but the sky was large and very high. The middle of the world was at the San Francisco Peaks, the highest peaks in Arizona, north of Flagstaff, and visible from all parts of Havasupai territory except in the deep tributary gorges of Grand Canyon. This visibility accounts for the belief that the San Francisco Peaks are central in Havasupai world concepts even though, geographically, they are near the southeastern corner of their former range.

Underground consisted of four levels, as did the sky. Shamans are reported to have seen these latter levels, which were inhabited by people with wings, sky people, *mi ä²bä²djih.*

The Havasupai recognized six directions, including the zenith and nadir. There existed a vague notion of an ocean to the west, probably learned from the Mohave who had traded with coastal people.

Of the neighboring tribes the Havasupai knew the Walapai, Hopi, Apache, Southern Paiute, and Navajo. An interesting denial of knowledge of the Yavapai perhaps results from the Havasupai consideration that, of all creatures, the Yavapai were farthest from a human category. Further, unless one makes specific separate inquiry, Havasupais often tend to equate the Yavapai and Apache. Tales of Apache raids in reality refer to Yavapai encounters. They knew of Zuni and Acoma, but did not visit Zuni or farther east. Knowledge of these pueblos came to them through the Hopi.

Southern Paiutes formerly visited and camped in Pai territory. Our informants reported that some would swim across the
Colorado River near Prospect Valley where access to the river
may be gained from either side of Grand Canyon. Paiutes also
crossed in the vicinity of Diamond Creek where a Southern Paiute
campsite, Ariz. G:3:1 in the Arizona State College Archaeological
Survey files, has been recorded at the junction of that stream with
the Colorado River and below there in the vicinity of Granite
Park where Walapai campsites and mescal pits, Ariz. G:3:2
(ASC), have been recorded. These visits included those during
which the Paiutes introduced the Pai to the 1890 Ghost Dance.

Hopis also frequented Havasupai villages and there was
considerable movement of both peoples on the trading route
extending along the south rim of Grand Canyon.

Sacred Places and Spirits

Shrines and sacred places were few, especially outside Cataract
Canyon. Spirits were thought to inhabit Gray Mountain on the
eastern boundary of their historic range. A certain rock formation
underlying the Coconino sandstone at the end of the Great
Thumb peninsula in Grand Canyon was visited to make rain. The
salt deposits on the Colorado River below the mouth of the Little
Colorado were used by the Havasupai but were not considered
sacred. The San Francisco Peaks and Mount Sinyella, an isolated
sandstone remnant on the esplanade northeast of Supai village,
were thought to contain spirits which, if appealed to, could produce rain. But people felt afraid to go too close to the sites. They
were considered dangerous, since visitors to them might cause too
much rain or strong winds that could blow people off the canyon
walls.

Virtually every spring known to the Havasupai contained
spirits. Offerings of tobacco, peaches, or dried corn were made to
these water sources, and menstruating women were cautioned
against visiting them, since the water might disappear. Prayer
sticks, however, were not used at springs, as was the Hopi custom.

Conception of the Soul

Leslie Spier indicated that the Havasupai believed that "Each human has a soul in his heart; . . ." Our consultants confirmed this, virtually denying a separate term for the soul. It was called "the heart" and "works inside with the blood." A person had only one soul. Beyond this, however, there was a vague concept of some powerful aspect coming from the air and sun which, together with the heart, was a condition of life. "When the heart quits, you know they died." We could elicit no additional data as to when or how the soul entered an individual except that it came from the east.

When a person died, the soul journeyed to the sky people. Shamans reported that the soul left the body through the pulse area in the throat. The soul went straight up in the air and then wandered around until it saw "that narrow path that leads to the place of the dead." Two lay consultants, however, remarked that the soul stayed with or near the body of a buried person if the body had been interred with the head to the west. This apparent discrepancy probably stems from the shamans' concern with the spirits and their exorcism. The souls of shamans depart for a separate place in the sky. If a person committed suicide his soul would go to the west to join those of all people who wanted to die. There was a spirit being in the west who was considered malevolent and who attempted to influence people to his cause. To the east was another spirit who attempted to counteract his western counterpart. These looked like humans but did not have human substance. The one in the east was white; the one in the west was black. When they quarreled, the eastern spirit made half the world white, and the western spirit made the other half black. They quarreled often over individuals, each trying to attract people to his sphere.

It was believed that at death a person became unconscious and had no knowledge of what was happening. However, after death, while the deceased was thought to know his identity, his relatives, and where he had lived, he would not remember his illness. After death, souls took either the form of a person or of a household pet such as a cat or a dog, and could return as ghosts. This usually happened at night. If a ghost attempted to return and

communicate with a close friend, the friend would become sick
and die. If ghosts appeared in a darkened form or "like a fire
burning red," they were considered more harmful. Occasionally
people saw ghosts of the dead walking by or heard them making
noise. The body below the waist appeared normal, but the upper
portions were without head or arms. It was wrong to try to touch
a ghost; one might become weak. If one cried out, one would fall
unconscious. A shaman would be called to sing for one who saw
a ghost. The shaman would walk over the area where the ghost
had been encountered in an attempt to learn why it had wanted
the person who saw it to become sick and die. The shaman then
would sing, urging the ghost to leave. Shamans also sang over the
patient. One informant, referring to an event that occurred about
1920, said that one evening when it was nearly dark he had seen
two persons standing by his house. At first he thought they were
neighbors, but noticed that they were dressed in white and had no
heads. It appeared as though smoke was coming from their necks.
He watched a short while and saw them "turn to nothing." The
next morning he went to a Walapai shaman, Dr. Tommy, from the
Pine Springs–Diamond Creek area. The shaman told him that he
also had seen the ghosts, and that one was a man who had died
not long before. The shaman had talked with the ghosts, who
indicated that they meant no harm. But the shaman ordered them
back to the grave. They were not seen again, and Dr. Tommy did
not sing over the patient.

    If one dreamed of a deceased person or "a dead horse you
used to keep," one would, in the dream, accompany the ghost
and eat with him. Upon waking, to prevent harm the person
would exhale audibly and forcefully while brushing the hands
away from the face and saying, "I don't want to go with you dead
people. Go away from me and stay away." This procedure was
repeated four times. If the individual became sick, a shaman was
called. During a dream a person's soul traveled around, returning
before waking. Therefore, a person should not be awakened suddenly since the soul might not have time to return.

    If men or women dreamed of sexual intercourse, it was
proper to relate it upon waking. The dream was told after one
exhaled and brushed one's hands away from the face four times.
If this was not done, one's back would stiffen or "something like
a young cottonwood tree will grow on your backbone so you

can't bend before middle age." It was dangerous if one could not remember the details of a sexual dream. Then it would "stay in the heart" and one could not counteract it. There was no danger in forgetting an ordinary dream.

If one dreamed of being in a precarious place, if awakened suddenly one must relate it and not keep it in the heart; otherwise either illness would occur or the spirit would fall from a cliff causing the person to be killed in the same way.

The Havasupai had but few other omens of impending death. If one heard an owl hooting during the day or late in the evening, it meant that a close relative was dying somewhere. The noise of a porcupine could indicate the same. As one consultant phrased it, "Those two are really proof, because we saw a porcupine in a tree where we camp out and go to bed. When it just got dark, when we thought we heard an owl say, '*h-hoo, h-hoo,*' then '*ow, ow, ow,*' we saw it was a porcupine. That was dangerous, so we took a gun, held sticks from the fire to see by, saw it by building up fire, and shot it. Just a few days later we met some boys who told us a close relative in Supai was dying. We were near Ashfork. We saw that it was proof."

If, while traveling at night, a red fire was seen burning far off, it meant that someone was dying somewhere. If a snake came inside a wickiup, someone was sick or had had an accident and would probably die. A husband was not supposed to kill a snake when his wife was pregnant because the baby's legs and arms would be weak and limber.

Should a man see a woman urinating or vice versa, one would die unless one said, "It's going to witch us. We don't want that."

Shamans and Illness

Formerly, a shaman could give his own spirit to a relative, or it could be inherited after the shaman's death. If it was given during life, the new shaman had to remain with the older for four nights. The older shaman sang over him in order that his spirit would become familiar with the initiate and remain with him. A "spiritual string" passed between the mouths of the two men; this, a part of the spirit, was swallowed by the initiate. It enabled the shaman to see over his patients' bodies and was thought to aid in the diagnosis and destruction of the illness. The new shaman, notwithstanding, then had to dream to acquire his power through songs. Otherwise the spirit would not remain with him.

Occasionally a man aspiring to be a shaman would pay for it. Dr. Tommy was paid a horse for his spirit.

The "string" referred to above was used in the following way: The shaman would first remove it from his mouth and exhibit it to the spectators. Then he would appear to insert it through the patient's head or throat for the diagnosis. Other shamans diagnosed by placing their hands or elbows on the mouth of the patient. They withdrew the illness this way also. Some then swallowed the sickness, others blew it away. Most, however, sucked the afflicted area of the body.

Rock Jones, a shaman when Spier worked with the Havasupai, often treated a patient by singing and pressing his hands on various portions of the patient's body. He stood up except while singing or shaking his gourd rattle. During Spier's study, Rock Jones was a weather shaman but later learned curing from his brother.

Diagnosis also was accompanied by singing special songs, which would be answered by the shaman's spirit, often in the guise of an old woman or a small boy who were sky people. The female spirit is *Gimní dem genwí va* (old woman living by herself) and the boy is *Hihman kai ij gen wí va* (little boy living by himself). He was thought to be her grandson. The woman lived in the west, the boy in the east. Each shaman had his own individual songs to attract his spirit. These were not given to a new shaman.

Another curing shaman received his power through a small bone that had been given to him from a cave. He then had a dream in which the bone talked to him and told him it would give him the power to become a shaman. He kept the bone for two years, at which time a Walapai shaman took it away on the pretense that it might otherwise be harmful to the Havasupai. However, the bone continued to appear in the Havasupai shaman's dreams and taught him curing songs.

The shaman who served as our informant had not been one during Spier's day. He began about 1931 or 1932 when he started dreaming about it. These dreams came to him not through his own desire, but because *Pagiýova*, a localized mythical culture hero wanted it. This happened at a time when his mother was ill. During his dreams he didn't see anyone, but heard an unidentifiable voice telling him what to do. Later, after he no longer heard the voice, the spirit became visible. In a dream the spirit took him through the air to Red Butte, south of Grand Canyon village, where the informant had been born. He saw the spirit in human form approaching on a white horse. The spirit dismounted and shook hands, saying, "I am not a dead person, I am a man just like you. Do you have any relatives who have died?" When the informant replied in the negative, the spirit said, "A relative of yours died and went northeast. Then he turned south and he is over at my place." Our informant thought, "Maybe it's my brother," but he didn't tell the spirit. The spirit then said, "There will be a new kind of sickness that will come to everybody, white men and Indians. The sickness comes from the war they are having across the ocean. It will come to the Indians first." When the spirit first shook hands he made "white lightning" enter the informant's upper left arm and this later aided his power. The spirit then taught him to sing power songs and instructed him in shamanistic ritual. He learned many curing songs and had to remember their meaning. If he forgot, he would die. It took five or six years for him to become competent. It is unknown whether the consultant had past contacts with Navajo singers, who traditionally rode white horses.

After he had become a shaman he visited the eastern spirit being often, and thought he had been adopted by it. The spirit had made four hands. Only the first of these hands, a right one, was benevolent; the other three were left and were harmful. Sick people were "transported" by this particular shaman to the place in the east where the hands were. If the patient chose the first hand to shake he would recover; otherwise the illness would remain.

On one dream journey the spirit on horseback took our informant to one of the highest of the San Francisco Peaks. It was very steep and the spirit told him to walk around it, stepping carefully in footholes. Under the ground he could hear a strong wind humming as though it were far away. He put out his hand and patted down the top of the peak, saying, "I'm not here looking for trouble. I came here for a good reason. I came here for a lot of drinking water." The wind decreased and our informant

awakened, not knowing why he had uttered these words except
that it was upon instruction from the spirit.

In his next dream he heard a voice and believed he had also
shaken his gourd rattle. Then many short red pieces of lightning
came out of the ground and lay motionless on its surface. The
lightning said, "You have brought me out of the ground." Our
informant reported that the lightning did something to him, that
he arose in the air carrying his rattle and went to the north side of
Bill Williams Mountain. There he saw two tall slabs of sandstone
so high they reached far into the sky. He stood on top of one of
these and heard a voice from the southwest saying, "I know you
are a medicine man. I don't know what kind. You try every trick.
You go around to all the places. I am going to test you." The
shaman put out his left arm, where his power was, and made a
slanted rock ramp with dirt underneath from where he was standing down to the ground. He walked along this until he came to a
place that had high, red rock walls in a V shape. Then he said, "It
has been hard for me going around. You want to test me. I want
to see you go my way and follow where I have walked on this
rock." The voice did not respond and the shaman thought it was
unable to follow him.

Then he walked in the direction from which the voice had
come and he arrived at a village that contained a long, straight
row of "cabins." In each were two women. Another shaman, rec-
ognizable to our informant, appeared and preceded him into one
of the houses. There he sat between the two women and put his
arms around them. Our consultant was angry and said, "I don't
know what kind of man you are. I'm not going after ladies. I'm
looking for a powerful spirit." Whereupon he left and traveled
easterly until he came to two rock walls parted like a V with a
plateau on top. He saw "a smoke of clouds" on the plateau. From
this smoke there issued various strange types of birds all in a line.
This smoke tried to bring about illness and had power like a spirit.
A voice from the smoke said that the shaman had persevered and
would be able to cure sickness. The shaman awakened at this
point, but continued to repeat this dream in his curing songs.

Other spirit helpers came to him in other dreams. For
example, one night our consultant dreamed of a bird that said,
"All my cousins, I don't know which direction they have gone
to." Before the shaman realized what was happening, he felt him-

self flying to the south until he finally came to earth near Rose Well within the eastern range of the Walapai. He stood on top of a big hill but could not see the bird. Shortly he saw a man standing in front of him but facing east. From the right side of the man's body white lightning "about the size of a stovepipe" shot toward the sun. The man said, "This is the lightning—powerful medicine—that cures any illness." Then he showed our consultant where the bird that he owned lived, and said, "When you sing, you must call the names of the bird, its nest, the cottonwood tree, and everything I show you." They then traveled north a short distance to a place where ice was like a mirror. The man told the shaman that the ice, "like a window that looks many directions," would aid him in diagnosing a patient's illness. At this point the shaman awakened. Later he sang of this man as "the man who is standing up alive." In his dream the man had not revealed any other name.

On still another occasion the shaman dreamed that he heard a voice calling plainly and repeatedly, "Come here. Let's fight each other." This was a voice from the north, which told the shaman, "I'll return four times and that will be the end of my life." At first the shaman didn't answer, but finally replied, "My lives are eight." He heard the voice no more, but found himself in the air traveling north. He landed where there were many people speaking different languages. Some had squeaky voices like bats and others imitated various birds. One bird told him to go to Rain Tank a few miles south of Grand Canyon village. When he arrived there in his dream, he followed two tracks leading east. Soon he came to two tall blue rocks. He climbed the south one and, halfway up, found some barely visible pictographs that appeared old. He blew on them four times until the pictures became clear. They depicted many kinds of animals and some humans. The shaman proceeded to the top of the rock where one of his spirits told him to look at some plants growing on the ground below. The spirit told him that formerly the plants were edible. Then the shaman was transported through the air northeasterly toward Cameron (a trading post on the western Navajo Reservation where U.S. Highway 89 crosses the Little Colorado River, near the northeastern edge of Havasupai territory). Near there he saw many people coming from underground, and also talking an unintelligible language. This time there were more people than he had seen in the north. The shaman waited until they were all on the surface. They spoke (but the informant couldn't explain his sudden understanding) and told him, "Over by the San Francisco Peaks there is something to fight sickness, to drive it away and conquer it." This proved to be small red rocks, about a foot long, and cylindrical "like a baby bottle." The shaman gathered these and tied them in cloth. Then the people advised him to take one more, a smooth opaque white one that could be rubbed on patients' chests to eliminate sickness. The shaman returned with his rocks to Rain Tank and told "sickness that he didn't want it to be going around." The ground around turned white as though it were snow covered. The shaman awakened but later reported that he had felt the dream had not been complete.

The first spirit he had seen mounted on the white horse continued to come in dreams, teaching him new songs until he knew about twenty, each for a different illness. Errors in singing them would harm the patient. However, if the shaman realized his error he could correct it by beginning the song again. These songs followed a definite sequence, outlining the case history of the patient. The number of songs also increased in direct proportion to the severity of the illness. For one patient, our informant sang six songs and repeated them seven times on each of four nights. Patients were sung over for four nights if the illness was severe or if the spirit of a deceased shaman was suspected of attempting to exert counterinfluence to the cure. In the example under consideration, the spirit of Rock Jones, a relative, was under such suspicion.

The first night the shaman was not able to diagnose the illness. Even though he sang all night he made no attempt to contact his spirit until the second evening. If a shaman wished to communicate with his spirit he did so only at the end of the night's singing. He put his own spirit, plus that of a female, in the patient. The female spirit, one of the sky people, never dies and is thought to remain inside the patient so long as the shaman desires. In this instance the female spirit was invoked because the patient was a woman. If a woman wished to die the female spirit stayed with her a long time. Under other circumstances the shaman would invoke only his own spirit, which would remain inside the patient only until the conclusion of the treatment. Sometimes it would be inserted from the shaman's mouth, at

other times from the head or arm. Our informant used both techniques, placing his hand on top of the patient's head and telling
the spirit to enter, as well as blowing and sucking on the patient's
throat. Additional sucking could be accomplished on the afflicted
part of the body.

Various illnesses assumed specific form and color as they
became apparent to the practitioner. These would first take on
false, undiagnostic shapes in an attempt to trick the shaman, and
were thought not to reveal their true form until the last song. For
example, pneumonia was round, smoke gray, and mixed with
blood. Flu was round but blue and silver. Less serious illnesses
were reported to appear to the shaman in the form and color of
playing cards: visions of Queens and Jacks would appear to flash
on and off the patient's chest.

Occasionally a shaman wore eagle-down feathers in his hair
while curing. These were tied at the back of the head and hung
loosely. Shamans also put feathers and white paint on the
patient. The paint, white clay obtained near the village, was
applied in dots or lines in varying designs according to the illness.
No special garments or other ceremonial appurtenances were
worn by either shaman or patient.

Shamans usually practiced alone, but four lay singers would
sometimes assist. They did not know the words of the shamans'
songs, but hummed the tune or rhythm. These assistants would
participate only during the first song, which was repeated four
times. If a patient was considered very ill, however, the relatives
might request an additional shaman to sing. Once when our
shaman consultant was ill, he asked three other shamans, including a Walapai, to sing for him. However, he was not cured and,
according to him, his own spirit told him to consult an Anglo
physician. Shamans usually did not have the power to cure themselves or close relatives.

Our lay informants denied that females became shamans,
although they reported one formerly among the Walapai. This is
in agreement with Spier and Kroeber. Havasupais frequently had
the Walapai shamaness sing for them when they were visiting that
area. However, our shaman informant knew of one elderly Havasupai woman who sang over sick people. She did not effect cures
by herself, but sang with male shamans at their request.

Within the lifetimes of our consultant no shamans had been

killed for failing to effect a cure. An aboriginal pattern for killing a shaman seems clear, however. One shaman who lost a patient, and who was suspected of having used a malevolent spirit, was hung by his neck from a mesquite tree while brush piled under him was ignited.

It was thought that pictographs painted on cliff walls were done by shamans with the intent to harm someone. Those in a rock shelter in Cataract Canyon a few miles upstream from the village were considered especially dangerous. The site was a former Havasupai occupation shelter and has been recorded in the archaeological survey of the Museum of Northern Arizona as NA 7306. My lay consultant who took me to it denied any knowledge of the paintings. Our shaman consultant believed that one individual who lost his vision did so because he frequently passed by this point. It should be noted, however, that these pictographs are along the formerly heavily traveled Topocoba trail to the plateau.

It was considered improper for shamans to request payment for their services, although relatives of the patient usually profferred gifts within a month of the treatment. Tanned buckskin, Navajo blankets, or food were typical gifts. It would appear from our data that the shaman considered this an act of goodwill rather than specific payment for his services.

Weather shamans had less power; usually they did not acquire a spirit. Spier noted that they "obtained power by dreaming of clouds, thunder, lightning, and of great rain and hailstorms." Rock Jones dreamed of clouds that talked to him. He could see the clouds but could not feel them. He could call them to come near, but only if he was alone. Later, when he became a curer, the same clouds helped him to cure spider and snakebites. Weather shamans did not dance for rain. They sang alone, sometimes before an audience.

Before Rock Jones died he didn't leave his cloud power to anyone. The Havasupai have not had a weather shaman since, although our shaman consultant believed the power could still come to one of Jones's descendants. Another consultant, however, referred to Rock Jones as a malevolent person who had witched and killed many people. Upon his death, his power was consigned to the Yavapai, enemy people, so that it could never return to harm anyone.

Game shamans also were known to the Havasupai. Before

extended hunting forays, the shaman would sing special songs calculated to quiet deer and prevent them from running when hunters approached. These were sung at night and repeated four times. Their content involved not only information about the habits of the animal, but also that the hunters were sorry for killing the game needed to assuage their hunger. Locations the hunters intended to visit were also mentioned. Successful hunters frequently prayed to the sun to shine brightly so the deer could be seen. The sun was thought to "own" the animals.

Game shamans could lure only certain species. *Čik pániga,* one of three remembered by our consultants, was thought to have power over deer and mountain sheep, but not antelope. While antelope abounded in the upland regions of Havasupai territory, they were hunted only in time of dwindling food supplies. There existed a belief that if antelope hair got on the meat it would bring stomach cramps to the eater. None of these men were curers. They gained their power through dreaming of specific animals and were not instructed by other shamans. Following a successful hunt, the game shaman usually was given a hindquarter or a section of the ribs, but this gift was not mandatory.

Some consultants believed that diarrhea was brought on through eating spoiled meat. Game shamans, therefore, frequently were thought to be effective in curing that malady. The so-called "diarrhea songs," no longer remembered, referred to unspoiled, fat meat and the desire people had for it. No rattle accompaniment was used with these songs, which were usually repeated at least twice, though not always from the beginning. The songs were sung over both adults and children. During these songs the shaman (or, in the case of a baby, its father) would gently massage the patient's abdomen in an attempt to locate flatulent areas. The singer also would take ashes from the fire, rub them between his palms, and blow them to the east, exhaling audibly as he did so. This action was thought to remove any accompanying pain.

Another specialized shaman was one who could cure the bites of snakes, scorpions, and black widow spiders. Particular songs, no longer recalled, were sung to ease pain and to lull the patient to sleep. The shaman also cut the wound with an obsidian or flint blade and sucked the afflicted area. On such occasions, the shaman did not invoke his spirits. The songs, repeated four times, were considered sufficient.

Of some interest are the nonpower-giving dreams of shamans. Our shaman consultant recalled several that appeared to him to be distinct from the dreams of lay people. They revealed data concerning the soul, life after death, and cosmology. Specifically, he denied an Anglo belief in heaven and hell because, in his dreams, he frequently saw the dead nearby rather than in the sky or elsewhere. He dreamed about deceased persons, both those whom he knew, such as his mother's mother, and those about whom he had only heard. Once he dreamed of a "white man" who lived beside the sun in the east. This man told people how to prosper and to obtain good clothing and land. In the west was a "dark man" who gave bad advice. These two quarreled frequently about what each told the Havasupai. After one such argument the "dark man" tried to pull all the people in a dark place enclosed by a high wall but the "white man" shone light upon it.

The shaman also dreamed often of traveling through the sky. On these occasions he saw no sky people—only uninhabited deep canyons.

Once he dreamed of going under the ground. The earth was coal-black, as were some people he saw there. He was afraid and wanted to faint, but with a long stick he removed a lid covering the shaft through which he had entered and he hurried away.

On another occasion he dreamed of a wind that carried him to the south "where the air was good to breathe." On a mountain he saw a man who was a good talker. He also was "white" and "looks like a Supai, talks Supai." This man asked the shaman why he always traveled around through the sky. The shaman didn't answer but awakened.

Concepts of Disease and Illness

Virtually all sickness was believed to have been brought about by malevolent dreams, sorcery, or other supernatural causes.

Psychologically upsetting dreams, especially those involving the possibility of death or loss of the soul, were considered especially harmful. If the individual revealed the general nature of his dream, his family would consult a shaman, who would then sing in an interrogatory fashion to ascertain specific details. The practitioner could exorcise the evil either by sucking intrusive objects from the patient or, through songs, ensure the return of the soul. If a person repeatedly dreamed of a deceased relative, it was believed that the dead person wanted to take the living away. This was particularly true in the case of an individual who died while learning shamanistic powers.

Shamans were often thought to be sorcerers who could produce illness either in others or in their own immediate families. Anyone who believed a shaman was harboring a particular grudge against him might come under such a spell. A deceased shaman could cause inanimate objects such as rocks, water, ground, air, and the sun to make people ill. Bone fractures also were thought to have been caused by evil shamans, either living or dead. Other shamans could effect cures in the same way they counteracted dreams. Fractures were usually set by the shaman before he began to sing.

The vision of a ghost could cause serious illness or death, although this was not invariable. Such visions tended to afflict older persons more than children. Further, not all ghosts were considered malevolent. Again, shamans, by ascertaining the identity of the ghost, could rid the individual of the malady.

Shamans themselves could become ill if they made errors in their cures of others or in other ways disobeyed instructions from their spirits. One case brought to our attention involved a shaman who, in an effort to suck a foreign object from a patient, made a mistake. It was reported that he became sick almost immediately and bled from the mouth. (The consultant was unaware of the ill shaman's medical history of tuberculosis.) Another shaman was called upon to effect a cure.

Frequent cases of diarrhea in children were thought to result from the parents' eating spoiled meat or meat from an animal that had been killed by a predator. Shamans had to be told the particulars before attempting to cure.

Preventive Medicine

The Havasupai had few concepts of preventive medicine. Strips of porcupine skin with the quills attached occasionally were worn on a hat or on the back of the shirt over the shoulder to ward off illness. A sharp piece of obsidian worn as a pendant was thought to be similarly effective. No decoctions were drunk, no physical exercise was indulged in, and no precautionary ceremonies were employed as preventive medicine. No care was taken to hide hair or nail parings nor was any significance attached to them. Babies' hair, however, was not discarded on the ground; should a bird make a nest from it the infant might die.

Medicinal Therapy and Contraceptives

Only a few plants and minerals were thought to have therapeutic value, and these were used primarily for minor dermatic inflammations. Sap from stems of the willow was applied to pimples. Grass ashes were sprinkled on any type of open sore. A pinch of salt, either dry or dissolved in water, was blown on sore eyes. Needles of the Douglas fir were boiled and the liquid drunk to stem excessive bleeding from an injury or during menstruation. Tea made from the leaves of *Ephedra* or juniper was taken for diarrhea.

We were unable to obtain any data concerning the importation and use of peyote. All consultants denied it. Flora Iliff, discussing the period just prior to 1900, also indicated that the Havasupai "apparently had no knowledge of peyote." Her illustration entitled "Under the tent the peyote cult will hold its all-night service, followed by a feast," seems not to have been photographed in the Havasupai country. Although the Walapai might once have experimented with peyote, the movement did not last and is not present among them today. Jimson weed was not used in any way according to most of our consultants, although Spier reported its sporadic use by lay persons if not by shamans. One individual, however, remarked that the juice from the leaf of jimson weed was rubbed on red ant bites.

To prevent conception a woman could urinate on red ants, eat the meat of cottontail rabbit, antelope, or ground squirrel while menstruating, or drink a solution of water in whch pack rat feces had been soaked. Women could conceive more easily if they ate prairie dog meat. Abortion could be induced by carrying heavy objects or by having one's husband step on one's back during the early months of pregnancy.

The Sweatlodge and Its Therapeutic Functions

We were unable to elicit data concerning the introduction of the sweatlodge to the Havasupai. It is probable that they adopted it from the Southern Paiute or, less probably, from the Navajo. We have no archaeological knowledge of its earliest use. The legend included below that Wolf and Coyote built the first one is of no help.

Our information concerning sweatlodge construction agrees generally with that of Spier. No ceremony was involved in building the small domed structure. Several men cooperated, although women sometimes assisted. Openings faced east, with the area inside and just to the left of the door provided for the hot rocks, in contrast to Navajo sweatlodges where the rocks are always to the right of the entry. All present Havasupai sweatlodges are dirt-covered, as are those of the Navajo. Spier noted that in his day the framework was covered only with layers of blankets and buffalo robes, but that F. H. Cushing mentioned a covering of dirt. Actually, Cushing also saw them "closely covered with blankets." Iliff, in a photograph taken around 1900, illustrates a used sweatlodge without a dirt covering, as does George James, and it would seem that this certainly was the more common. Our consultant indicated that the dirt-covered sweatlodge became universal around 1920.

Spier reported the size as "2 m. in diameter and 1.3 m. high set over a circular pit 20 cm. deep." One that Smithson and I frequented was approximately the same: 2.05 m in diameter; 1.07 m high at center; 75 cm high in area where participants sat; 53 cm high at entry; 75 by 50 cm area of heated rocks; 50 cm depth of pit.

While the sweatlodge serves in some respects as a "clubhouse" for the men, it also involves certain therapeutic and ritual functions. In former times, persons who had been wounded would receive part of their treatment in the sweatlodge, and even now individuals with broken bones and various aches, sprains, and pains are treated there. A wounded man would enter the sweatlodge with a shaman and two others, four being the ideal total number prescribed for each use of the lodge. They would enter backwards, the shaman taking his place nearest the heated rocks and the water that was sprinkled on them. Frequently, sweet-smelling herbs or leaves would be hung in a bundle above

the rocks, and the floor of the lodge covered with willow or cottonwood branches. The shaman would sing a song and repeat it
four times, although, if the shaman were not present, another
man who knew the songs could act in his place. Spier indicated
that sweatlodge songs were sung not by a shaman but by an old
man. Our data indicate that either could participate.

At the conclusion of each song, the shaman usually would
place his mouth on the afflicted portion of the patient's body and
forcibly blow his overheated breath on the area. Hand pressure
also was applied in the belief that forced movement of the blood
would work the heat into the painful spot.

Songs used in the sweatlodge were not to be sung outside it.
They were different from those a shaman learned in his dreams,
but were, nevertheless, not to be taken lightly. The entire procedure was repeated four times. The men remained in the sweatlodge fifteen to twenty minutes each time and, in the intervals, lay
on the hot sand in front of the entry. Rubbing the body with sand
was thought to aid in the removal of the affliction, as was the
heat; drinking copious amounts of water before and after the
sweatbath was believed to "clean out the body." At the conclusion it was customary, although not mandatory, to bathe in the
river. Even when a shaman was not present, the man who entered
first would dip his right hand in the water, sprinkle the hot
stones, and speak aloud about how the heat, water, rocks, and
steam would remove the aches from their bodies. Others would
respond with the term *hánaga*, good, whenever reference was
made to good health or the removal of illness. Then the initial
man would begin his song and the others would accompany him,
humming if they did not know the words.

It is clear that the attitude toward the curing ritual in the
sweatlodge is more casual than that at other shamanistic rites.
Cures may or may not be effected. Iliff detailed a case of an ill
child whom shamans refused to treat. The boy's parents had him
placed in a sweatlodge where he was sung over by two laymen.
Shortly after, he recovered.

It was and is customary to take sweatbaths almost every day
in the summer, usually in the late afternoon. In the winter, the fre-
quency was reduced to two or three times a month.

Men and women, whether ill or not, should avoid sexual
intercourse for four nights before using the sweatlodge. If one vio-

lated this prescription it was thought blindness and excessive facial wrinkles would occur in middle age. Both sexes may avail themselves of the sweatlodge simultaneously, although it is customary for a woman to enter with her husband. Both sexes avoid exposing themselves unduly. Men wear loincloths, today fashioned from burlap; women wear slips, which they lower to the waist when inside. Children also are permitted to use the sweatlodge with adults, but do not do so frequently. Smaller children usually are permitted its use only when ill, and a sick baby would be placed outside near the entry while someone inside sang for its recovery. Some of our consultants believed, however, that in former times the sweatlodge was restricted to adults, especially those suffering from pain and soreness occasioned by hard work and long horseback or foot trips.

Pregnant women and their husbands were forbidden the use of the lodge because of the belief that the fetus would sweat and "become ill," or that the infant would be born blind. Menstruating women and their husbands also were advised against taking sweatbaths, although this taboo could be lifted if a woman suffered severe menstrual pain. On these occasions the woman would hold a small twig of "squaw-bush" (*Rhus trilobata*) in her mouth to prevent her from becoming wrinkled or blind in later years. Care was taken to keep the menstrual discharge from contaminating the structure. Should a man and woman using the lodge together be discovered in sex play, the structure would be abandoned.

That participation in Havasupai sweatbaths is refreshing and relaxing has been noted by all ethnologists who have experienced them. Smithson and I, independently, noted the same reactions. Unaccustomed to the intense heat, which Smithson recorded as ranging between 118° and 157° F, we felt weakness and sensations of searing of the skin, lungs, and nostrils. But once we were outside, and even while subsequently bathing in the river (water temperature 65° F) a refreshing feeling ensued. My own sweatbaths usually were taken following long, tiring horseback trips.

Death and Funeral Customs

When an individual was suspected of being near death, relatives tried to stay nearby. In the past a song, *mätabílyih*, sometimes was sung, either by the ill person or by a close relative who had requested permission from the patient. This was a preparatory act and insured that the individual would "keep the song" after he had died. But this is no longer done, and no one now remembers any of the songs. Wailing also began before death.

At death, relatives washed the corpse and dressed it in clean clothes. A blanket was wrapped around the body and sewn together leaving an opening only for the face. Within twenty-four hours it was cremated or, in more recent times, interred. "Crys" or mourning rites, without dancing, were held at any time convenient for the majority of survivors. Today the Mohave mourning ceremony has been adopted, not only after the death of an individual, but, through acculturation, annually on May 30, Memorial Day.

Spier reported the last cremation twenty-five years before his study, but our consultants referred to two cremations in the winter of 1919 (when the ground was frozen hard). According to Alfred Whiting, Sinyella's son was cremated in 1897, Chief Navajo was buried in 1898, and Rock Jones was cremated in the late 1920s. When Edward Curtis visited the Havasupai he reported only interment of the dead. Infants were not cremated in fear that the mother would become barren. The deceased's head was pointed to the north, less frequently south or west, and never to the east in fear that the latter position would guarantee return of the ghost. Burial in rock crevices or in caves was common, although today all are buried in a cemetery below the village.

Prior to the adoption of the Mohave funeral ceremony with its accompanying dancing, when a corpse was ready to be either cremated or interred, a lone speaker would stand near the head and, addressing the deceased, tell it that those still alive wish it had not died, that it was nevertheless going to a better place with better food and water, and that the living must await their time.

Spier was correct in indicating that the first Mohave mourning songs were used at a funeral in 1919, although some Havasupai had begun to learn them as early as 1914. At the time some Mohaves and Chemehuevis visited Havasupai and sang them at a "pow-wow." Later, the Havasupai learned others from the Walapai. The use of the Mohave dance at funerals may not have begun until as late as 1943.

Since a contemporary Havasupai funeral ceremony has not been reported upon in detail, we shall describe the one that

Carma Lee Smithson observed in 1951. The following straightforward description of a comparatively recent Havasupai funeral was recorded with no attempt at interpretation. The songs and dance steps all are of Mohave origin, adopted by the Havasupai through the Walapai. Yet such ceremonies, as well as the annual mourning rite, continue to be a serious, deeply emotional part of Havasupai religion.

The Funeral of Mexican Jack

Mexican Jack died of tuberculosis at Grand Canyon on July 29, 1951, in his seventy-seventh year, as nearly as could be ascertained. He was a widower, leaving two children. Throughout his life he had been well respected, and during his final illness received the well wishes of many visitors who were deeply grieved at his approaching death.

The day following his death, in Havasupai village, Alva Jones, a village "crier," made the public announcement in a five-minute oration in which he did not mention the deceased by name, referring to him as "that old man who was sick at Grand Canyon." He urged that the funeral be held in Supai and that the body be returned there for burial but indicated that the relatives would make the decision.

Since the surviving relatives did not wish to suffer the expense of bringing the body to Supai, burial was arranged at the Drift Fence (between Grand Canyon village and Topocoba Hilltop) where the Havasupai have for some years maintained a small cemetery.

Among the people in the canyon several were restless, especially at night, and some reported seeing the ghost of Mexican Jack. It was not felt that this apparition would be harmful, but that in wanting to talk to the living it could be potentially dangerous.

Mexican Jack was buried at the Drift Fence within a day or two with little ceremony.

On the afternoon of August 4, Arthur Kaska, whose house was just across a fence marking the public land used for recreation, mounted his horse and rode to the recreation area where rodeo practice was being held. From a position on horseback near the cow chute, he called a lengthy announcement to the effect that the funeral dance would be held that night. He urged everyone to attend and told them that the dance would be held in front of the house of Clark Jack, Mexican Jack's son.

By 8:30 P.M. a fire had been built in front of the house, and relatives of the deceased had begun to gather around it. Mark Hanna came and addressed the nonrelatives who were grouped nearby. He requested that someone from the audience act as a speaker to remonstrate with the relatives about weeping over the dead. There was no immediate response.

While Mark was talking, many other people arrived. It appeared that everyone had walked to the ceremony. No horses were to be seen that night or in the morning. (Havasupais, especially men and boys, usually ride everywhere—except to funerals and the annual round dance.)

Soon the wailing by relatives began and people piled gifts of clothing near the mourners. The relatives were standing together in a tight line, while others gathered in a huddle around them. All wept and wailed aloud, "a-a-a-a-oh-oh-oy-oy-oy-oy-oy." Not everyone repeated this precisely, and individual variation occurred in forming the sounds, pitch, and repetition. Some people stood around for several minutes before joining the mourners, although gradually most of them joined the group, placing their right hands on a mourner's left shoulder as they wailed.

This initial wailing and emotional display lasted for ten or fifteen minutes. Then Mark Hanna made a speech to the relatives, advising them to grieve now and then to forget the dead and turn their thoughts to the living. Women stood with heads bowed and shoulders drooped. During the speech they occasionally broke out in low wailing almost like a song, but softly, so they could still hear what was being said. Men, too, stood with bowed heads and hats pulled down so that the brims hid their faces. Certain individuals displayed more emotion than others. One boy's shoulders shook as he was wracked with sobbing, while others merely made the appropriate sounds. Clark Jack wailed in a rather high, thin voice, while others, notably Louis Sinyella, had full voices that produced musical sounds even in the wail.

After Mark's speech, Clark spoke, extolling the virtues of his father and his love for him. He recounted his feelings when the hospital tests indicated that his father would not live long.

Both speeches, especially Clark's, were delivered in quavering tones, the men being overcome by emotion so that some words broke or came out in a "squeak." Tears ran down their faces. Clark's speech was an emotional experience such as most people would deliver if they tried to speak at the funeral of a beloved parent. It was a dignified and genuine display of a man's feelings in a ritual, culturally determined, and approved pattern.

While this last talk was being delivered, Teddy and some others, boys and men, set three posts in the ground and nailed boards from the top of one to the other, and from it to the corner of a small storeroom. On these they spread out the clothing donated for Mexican Jack. On the center post they hung a pair of new chaps. Then chairs were brought from the Episcopal mission church and placed in two rows facing each other in front of Clark's house.

Mark and Arthur took places on the opposite side of the fire facing east between the two rows of dancers. The male dancers faced south. Those with rattles—Lemuel, Louis, and Teddy—took their places, and were joined by Dan and Floyd. These all kept their same places throughout the night. Toward morning James, with his rattle, sat next to Teddy on the east end of the line. The identity of dancers at the west end changed occasionally. Most of these were young boys, including Neil Uqualla (almost twelve years old), who participated most of the night.

The men began singing and stood up for the first dance before any women took their places. Then Mecca and Faye went over and danced with them. They stayed at the west end of the women's line all night. After several dances, Hazel and Nettie took the two remaining chairs facing the five men who were then dancing.

James Wescogame stood apart with his rattle. First he sat near Arthur and Mark, who were singing duets accompanied by Mark's rattle. Later they were joined by Hardy and Alfred in the same area. Soon James moved to a chair behind the women's line at its west end and faced east. He was joined by Andrew, who was a good singer and appeared to be learning the songs. James remained in that position all night except for about two hours when he joined the men dancing.

Two songs, and sometimes three, were sung simultaneously during most of the night. The words, tunes, and rhythms differed

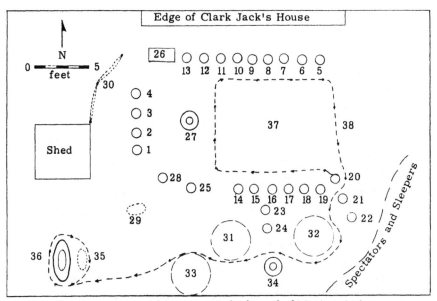

Arrangement of mourners at the funeral of Mexican Jack

1. Arthur Kaska, shaman
2. Mark Hanna, in charge, some-
   time shaman
3. Assistant to 1 and 2
4. Assistant to 1 and 2
5. Ed Hamidreek alternating with
   James Wescogame, dancers
6. Teddy Crook, dancer with rattle
7. Louis Sinyella, dancer with
   rattle, leading singer
8. Lemuel Paya, dancer
9. Dan Hanna, dancer
10. Floyd Putesoy, dancer
11. Neil Uqualla, dancer
12. Andrew Manakaja, dancer
13. Bela Wescogame, dancer
14. Mecca Uqualla, dancer
15. Faye Paya, dancer
16. CLS
17. Virginia, dancer
18. Nettie Putesoy, dancer
19. Hazel Crook, dancer
20. Gertrude, dancer
21. Margaret, dancer
22. Juana Burro, dancer
23. James Wescogame, solo singer
    with rattle; second position
24. Assistant to 23

25. Clark Jack, son of deceased,
    mourner
26. Coffee table
27. Fire
28. James Wescogame, first posi-
    tion
29. Where guests piled clothing
    gifts for the deceased
30. Rock on which clothing was
    displayed all night
31. Position of mourners during
    initial wailing
32. Position of mourners during
    wailing and round dance
    about 2:00 A.M.
33. Position of mourners and
    shaman during final wailing,
    round dance, and burning of
    offerings
34. Fire
35. Where clothing and posses-
    sions of deceased were piled
    while being thrown on fire, 36
36. Fire in which clothing was
    burned
37. Dance area
38. Line of dancers and direction
    of movement

for each, but each singer appeared not to pay attention to or be disrupted by the other two. When Mark and Arthur gave a speech between their songs their voices could not be heard, except by those seated closest to them, because of the noise of the other singers. Occasionally all would be silent at the same time. Then Joe Jones and several others would call out, "*Hánaga, Hánaga*" (good, good). Each of the three singers had a certain series of songs to sing, and there was a prescribed order to be followed. Mistakes were not considered harmful; sometimes the same song was delivered twice in succession. Each song consisted of one line repeated over and over thirty to fifty times. Those of James and the other team had more words and variety but took about the same time to sing. All those vocalized by the dancers during the first half of the night had the same time and dance steps. During the second half these were varied, with a new rhythm being used for every third or fourth rendition. Finally, for the last two dances, songs were sung which changed from one time to another, also requiring a shift in the steps. The most common dance step, wherein males and females in the two lines moved toward each other, involved a rhythmic shuffle by short steps, twelve forward starting on the right foot and twelve backward, also leading with the right foot. Louis Sinyella started each song for the dancers. Then the men sang it for several minutes, at which juncture their voices rose as they stood up together to move forward to the women's lines. As the two lines moved back and forth the men with rattles would accompany the singers, changing, near the end, from a continuous forward movement of the forearm in a short beat to a sideways motion involving the wrist in a more rapid beat. Once or twice when they did this, always when they were advancing, they stood shuffling in place near the women's side, repeating the song two or three times before continuing to dance several minutes more. There appeared to be no signal to let the women know when the dance would end, and a few times the women followed the men to their side and were left standing when the men sat down. The women would giggle and run quickly to their chairs.

On the whole, behavior of participants and spectators was respectful. Children occasionally moved around, but most slept throughout the funeral. At times, however, some of the young people in groups near the perimeter of the dance area talked and laughed as they drank coffee, and adults in the ceremony seemed not to pay close attention to the speeches.

A similar Walapai funeral that I (Euler) attended at Hackberry, Arizona, in the summer of 1956 was far less subdued. There was much drinking on the part of the younger men and women who attempted to compete with the adult dances by singing and dancing "rock and roll" music. Frequent harangues by the older mourners did little to curb these semi-intoxicated actions. Otherwise, the Walapai and Havasupai funeral ceremonies were identical.

Shortly after midnight the men sang a song with a different time, and the dance consisted of a step, a pause, and a shaking or shimmying of the body followed by a step with the opposite foot. The women swung their bodies in time to the music and joined hands all along the line, holding them slightly forward from the body. The men usually did not join hands, although one young boy danced the entire evening with his right arm draped around Neil's neck.

About 2:00 A.M., at the conclusion of one dance, Teddy danced sideways, using the round dance step. Followed by the men and then the women, he led the way around the area between the two rows of chairs, out the east end to the south. Here the dancers circled Clark and the other mourners who had stood up. After circling and singing several times, the dancers stopped and joined the wailing of the mourners. This was followed by a return of the dancers to their original position.

At 3:35 A.M. a rooster crowed. The sky was dark but filled with bright stars. There was no lightening of the eastern sky, but the people were stirred by a ripple suggesting relief. All night many had kept asking, "*Nya gal we?*" ("What is the time?")

About 4:30 several people became very drowsy during a long speech by Arthur. In this he spoke philosophically about the Havasupai pantheon and their native religion.

Around 5:00 A.M., when the sky was getting light, Guy Marshall and some other boys quickly dug a hole about 3-1/2 feet long, 2 feet wide, and 2-1/2 feet deep. They chopped some logs into short lengths and started a fire in it. Then someone came and asked Mack Putesoy to take charge of burning the clothing. Guy assisted him. Some boys removed the clothing from the display rack and piled it on the east side of the firepit on top of two pasteboard boxes and a suitcase containing Mexican Jack's per-

sonal clothing and possessions, on which Clark had sat throughout the night. Mack sprinkled this pile with a gallon of kerosene
before consigning it to the flames.

After the last regular dance, all the dancers, led by James
Wescogame and Teddy, began the round dance. They again moved
out of the dance area to the firepit and, with the round dance step,
circled the fire and clothing, with Mack and Guy inside the circle,
which moved to the left. Although Bela and one or two boys fell in
at the end of the line after the women, the number of dancers was
too few to form an enclosed circle around the fire area. They continued to dance until all the donated clothing was thrown on the
fire. The last item consumed was the new chaps. Then the dancers
stopped while the boxes and suitcase were emptied of their con-
tents, and moved over to join the mourners and Mark, Arthur, and
Allen, who had started to wail again when the fire was ignited.
Arthur cried long and emotionally, with tears streaming down his
face, his nose running, and saliva dripping from his mouth as he
leaned forward so as not to soil his clothes. He had frequently
wiped his tears away with his handkerchief during the night and
occasionally twisted it in his hands.

Clark kept wailing after the other mourners had stopped,
accompanied only by Louis Sinyella, who wailed loudly in a
deeper musical tone and a more ritual manner as he stood with
his hand on Clark's shoulder.

Before the fire had burned down, but at the end of the wailing, people left. Those who had been sleeping in scattered groups
around the area awoke and moved away. Only a few stayed
behind to cover the hole and the fire.

No participant had worn any costume or "badge of office."
Men and women wore their usual clothing with no attempt at
"dressing their best." A few men wore light overcoats or raincoats,
Several women wore short jackets or sweaters, while a few boys
wrapped themselves in blankets to ward off the early-morning
chill. The only special equipment used was the five rattles and the
donated clothing.

The following night Mark reported that he had seen Mexican Jack's spirit around the ceremonial area the previous evening,
and Teddy confided to Sidney that he had seen Mexican Jack's
apparition standing beside him as he danced, and later saw it in
the fire when the clothes were burned.

Dances

Spier described three dance formations for the Havasupai: the round dance, more social than religious; masked dances, probably in imitation of Hopi kachina impersonations; and the Mohave version of the bear dance. Our consultants confirmed the correctness of Spier's description of the round dance, and we can add but little data. Most of the songs were those invented by *Teyadjáva* although others were learned from Navajos and Southern Paiutes. The favorites to this day are those of *Teyadjáva* and *Gátágäma*. These are sung first and, if completed before morning, Paiute verses may be sung. Navajo songs are no longer part of the repertoire.

Certainly since at least the beginning of the twentieth century the round dance has been identified with the so-called peach or harvest dance held late in August or early in September. There are some hints that in the 1920s the performance still contained a residue of ghost dance elements, even though it probably antedates that nativistic movement. Apropos of this, an 1899 account in *The Arizona Graphic* gave a brief note of the ceremony:

> The Yava-Supais have an annual religious dance . . . and few white men have ever witnessed it. Superintendent McCowan [in 1899 at the Phoenix Indian School but in 1895 agent to the Havasupai] says he was a spectator at one of these ceremonies, but did not sit the programme through. The dance was seemingly interminable. The participants kept up a monotonous but energetic action, circling about a pole, to which was attached some "medicine." A chief kept spurring them on, and as they fell from exhaustion they were dragged from the ring and fresh dancers took their places.

The indication of influence from the ghost dance is due not only to the dance form with the inclusion of a center pole and the fact that some dancers seemed to be in a trance, but also that *Teyadjáva* and *Gátágäma* learned their songs from Southern Paiute ghost dance advocates. One of our consultants discussed this as follows:

> A group of Supais crossed the Colorado River and went to St. George [Utah] because they heard about the dance that makes the dead come alive again. *Teyadjáva* during the night took some Paiute songs and made them Supai songs. Supai Jack said that *Teyadjáva* didn't

dream these, but during the night a Paiute came to his bed and made this song and told *Teyadjáva*, "If you sing this song, you will find more songs added to it. I am the one that's giving songs to people that roam in this area."

Next morning, on their way home, *Teyadjáva* saw things like timber, mountains, waterholes, and springs. These things came into his heart and from that, the person he saw gave him more, night or day, round dance songs. He could make them up, some way, but didn't understand how.

From there he made up some danger songs like he heard thunder, lightning strike walls or tree; hits close to person; kills them. He made it into a song, lightning song, but he didn't want to use it; it's a danger song. He had many of those songs, but somehow he lost track of making better songs. He got sick by singing those things. Later on the man who had come to his bed kept watching wherever he goes, and he got witched from him, a medicine man or whatever he was. A medicine man sang over him and couldn't tell what was wrong. Finally he went to a Walapai medicine man to cure him. That medicine man said he saw two men: "You make these songs until you make better songs. They're keeping track to see if you make better ones. Somehow they have witched you. I can't cure you." From there he got worse and finally died. My father said when he went hunting with *Teyadjáva* he always saw things, or even at home, and always made new songs. He finally died with it.

Supai Jack and Bert Wescogame stood on either side of *Teyadjáva* in the round dance and learned songs from him. He told Jack and Bert not to keep the songs after he died, because he died from something serious in the songs and the same might happen to them later on.

After he died no one sang *Teyadjáva*'s songs for a round dance for quite a few years. Then M knew the songs. When he traveled to other tribes and they asked him for Supai songs, he sang *Teyadjáva*'s songs. Later they thought these might be good songs so now that's all they sing for a round dance.

I counted songs at the round dance when Supai Jack was leader. I counted thirty-one or thirty-two songs. I wanted to see how many songs Jack knew. Jack sang each song twice, so the series would last all night. These were *Teyadjáva*'s before *Gátágäma*'s were mixed with them. These are in Supai language. Jack said *Teyadjáva* had many more songs, but this was all Jack remembered.

Supai Jack and *Teyadjáva* lived together. They looked for horses and hunted together. That's how Jack heard him make up those songs right along.

They say he did not have a good singing voice. That's why he picked Jack and Bert, who both had good voices. He used to tell ladies not to get between him and Bert and Jack, as it spoiled the songs. He always wanted just the three in one place together. They were close enough so he could whisper and tell them which one came next.

There are, however, some indications that the Paiute songs used in the ghost dance of 1890 were different from those later made up by *Teyadjáva*:

> Men who went to St. George brought some Paiute songs home with them for ghost dance. Learned quite a few of them. At ghost dance they sang Paiute songs, did not sing *Teyadjáva*'s songs. In the village they sang Paiute songs. By that time *Teyadjáva* was also singing his songs. *Gätágäma* also was singing his own songs.

Apparently the Paiute ghost dance songs are almost forgotten and, hence, no longer used in the annual round dance. However, other nonmessianic Paiute songs are still in vogue.

We have some data relative to the association of the round dance and scalps: "If Supai killed an enemy, they cut the head off [sic] and hung it up on a pole and made a round dance around it." The songs for such an occasion were different from those delivered at other round dances, and their words concerned the warrior's good fortune in killing the enemy who had come to kill Havasupai. Our consultant referred to these as war songs. During these "victory dances" those whose relatives had been killed in an enemy engagement would dance around the pole shouting [not singing] and would shoot at the enemy's head with their arrows. They would shoot either from inside or outside the circle and repeat it every few minutes until the dance ended.

A sidelight concerning the claim that entire heads were taken is to be seen in one consultant's remembrance of a raid against the Yavapai.

> One time a chief and some other people wanted to follow their enemies [who had raided Havasupai village] to their homes beyond Bill Williams Mountain, south where the enemy usually came from. They came to a water hole where it looked like there had been many homesites. Quite a few Havasupai were in the party. They rested their

horses and watered there. Then they happened to see a man on a horse on a rise. They knew it was the enemy. He hollered and started down the other side. They knew his spotted horse was stolen from them. They rushed to their horses to follow him. Not far away they overtook him. They had good, fat horses but his was poor and run down. They killed this Apache man [for Apache, read Yavapai] opening his chest, spread it out and laid him flat on the ground. They took his head and tied it to the spotted horse's tail, high enough so they wouldn't lose it on the return trip. On this [north] side of Bill Williams Mountain in the timber the spotted horse was tired so they had to kill it—burned it. From there they packed the head on the tail of another man's horse. They came to Moki Tank. A family lived there. One old lady—her husband died—had a grown boy [who had been killed by Yavapai while out hunting]. They stopped there and put on a round dance with the head on a pole.

Spier reported that masked dances were discontinued twenty years before his study. These dances, undoubtedly adapted from the Hopi, were called *gidjiña yvma*^{k}? (kachina dance).

Anyone who wanted to put on such a dance could request permission from the subchiefs. Both men and women participated, according to our consultants, making a total of ten or more couples. I would be inclined, however, to agree with Spier, who indicated that only men danced. It is probable that, as in Hopi kachina dances, men impersonated women. The dancers formed a single file, men and women alternating. At a signal from the leader the men and women formed separate lines, and the dance leaders danced outside of the two columns. The dance leaders would move to the rear, followed by couples in turn, as Spier indicated, "much like a Virginia reel." Then one of the leaders danced again to the rear of the columns, and all of the participants returned to the single line, dancing away from the audience until they were out of sight. The dance step was similar to that of the Hopi, dancers moving their feet up and down in one spot, moving forward only when leaders started to the rear.

The songs were not Havasupai; our informants could not recall the language. The purpose of the dance was to bring rain. The participants pretended to be "weather people" who came to visit "these round dance people." A chief talked to them saying, "We are glad you came and brought us this food [corn, pumpkins,

melons carried by the women]. We need it. We like your weather.
When you return, tell your people we like your weather." Then,
in signs so as not to reveal his identity, the leader of the "weather
people" would nod affirmatively. He would point to the sky and
move his hands downward in a fluttering motion to indicate rain.
With two fingers straddling another finger and making a circular
motion he would indicate fat horses. With his hands describing a
circular motion over his stomach he indicated that it was filled
with food. Moving his hands upward he intimated growing grass
and crops.

Masks were not removed during the dance, in order to con-
ceal the identity of the participants, and children were led to
believe they came from another tribe.

At the conclusion of the dance two of the masked impersonators indicated that they wished to play games and engage in foot
races—an incorporation of the function of Hopi clowns. A good
runner from the audience would race them, attempting to gain
sufficient distance to prevent the masked racers from striking him
with whips. These were made of shredded yucca leaves tied
together and were three to four feet long. Another masked dancer
would stand at the finish line and distribute bread or peaches to
the audience while an unmasked person sprinkled white paint or
cornmeal on the dancers. This is obviously the counterpart of the
Hopi priest who acts as "father" of the kachinas during their per-
formances. The entire performance, dance and race, was repeated
four times.

Other clowning activities involved a pretense at anger on the
part of two of the masked men, often the leaders, who would
chase spectators or grab young girls in an attempt to dance with
them. On other occasions one of the masked figures would hold a
king snake and frighten the audience with it.

Spier's description and illustration of the masks were quite
accurate. The person sponsoring the dance prepared the masks
with some assistance from friends. They were made by doubling a
piece of canvas and sewing it into a sack. A face was painted on
the front. This involved geometric designs in black, red, and
white, although the colors had no special meaning. Openings for
eyes and mouth were cut into them. The masks of the two leaders
had leather tubes sewed to the mouth opening. Attached feathers

were tipped with down. Women's masks were characterized by only one or two feathers and were painted red and white in designs consisting of red vertical lines or crosses on the cheeks. Those depicted by Spier were more typical of those worn by men. Some women did not wear masks, but painted their heads white with a red circle outlining the face. This was exceptional, however. The associated costume of the women consisted of willow bark strips hung from a belt like a skirt worn over a dress. The masks of the male impersonators contained more feathers and were white with minor design elements in red and black. Occasionally horsehair was attached to simulate human hair. This was allowed to hang freely or was tied in a knot at the back. Men's costumes included willow branches and leaves encircling the waist to hide their rolled-up denim trousers. Their legs and bodies were painted white with black spots at random. These were intended to indicate raindrops. No lightning designs were utilized. Men also wore willow leaves in a ruff around the neck and carried willow branches in their hands, which they moved up and down in time with the dance rhythm. The men who distributed the food often wore cast-off women's clothing which they then discarded in a secreted dressing area.

Our consultants were in agreement that, aside from one attempt to hold the kachina dance in 1931 or 1932, the last had been portrayed in 1910, the year before the big flood. Prior to that it had been customary to hold one every year, usually in conjunction with the harvest round dance. The seemingly paradoxical action of having the rain dance at the harvest rather than during the earlier summer rainy season was explained by consultants who indicated that at the earlier date not enough fresh food would have been available for distribution to the audience. In all probability, the rain itself was not needed because of the perennial stream flowing through the fields, but the concept was retained along with the other obvious Hopi features. This dance certainly does not appear to be similar to the rain dance that A. L. Kroeber reported for the Walapai.

At least occasionally, a rain dance was held near two rock pinnacles along the Topocoba trail in a canyon upstream from the main village. These dances did not involve masked impersonators and were held only in dry years in an attempt to bring moisture

to the plateau. The rocks, *öʔwiʔgaᵗʰʔǵwä* (rock split apart) and
öʔihʔgaᵗč̣ʔ ǵwävʔ (wood piled up) were near a small spring, and
were considered rain "gods." No additional data concerning
these events could be learned.

Havasu Falls below Supai village. One of the four waterfalls on Havasu Creek. Robert Euler, September 1975.

A modern prefabricated house in Supai village beneath the sacred rocks Wi'geliva. Legend has it that the end of the Havasupai will come if the rock pinnacles ever fall. Robert Euler, April 1977.

A Havasupai pack train on the "Walapai Trail." This is the route most frequently used by Havasupai riders and tourist hikers to Supai village. Robert Euler, November 1977.

Tribal grocery store and U.S. Post Office in Supai village. Robert Euler, April 1977.

Southward aerial view of Supai village and farmlands. The sacred rocks of Wi'geliva are in the left center. Robert Euler, October 1959.

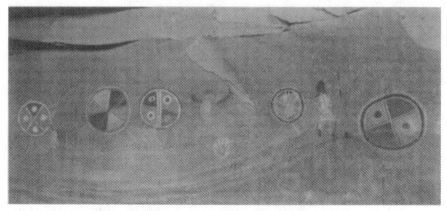

Historic Havasupai pictographs of hallowed symbols in a rock shelter in upper Havasu Canyon. Robert Euler, June 1959.

One of the most powerful late-nineteenth-century shamans, Rock Jones, who specialized in weather control, ca. 1895.

Navahu, Havasupai political leader in the late nineteenth century. So named because he was alleged to have killed a Navajo enemy. George Wharton James, ca. 1898, courtesy of Southwest Museum.

Spoonhead, a Havasupai man knowledgeable about religious customs. Carma Lee Smithson, August 1962.

Molly Mulgulu pauses to recollect during an interview in her wickiup about Havasupai religious and traditional life. Robert Euler, June 1959.

Molly Mulgulu with conical burden basket and twined tray. Robert Euler, November 1959.

Grinding seeds. Robert Euler, November 1959.

Lina Chick with a traditional cradle board she made. Carma Lee Smithson, August 1962.

Mamie Chick grinding seeds on a traditional Havasupai milling stone. A conical burden basket, typical of those made by Havasupai women, is at her left. Carma Lee Smithson, August 1962.

Allan Akaba, the last traditional Havasupai shaman and one of the authors' important sources of information about Havasupai religion. Carma Lee Smithson, August 1962.

Hmany gejaa (Managadja), Havasupai head chief from 1900 until his death in 1942. His name, given when he became chief, translates, "Leader of [his] children." George Wharton James, ca. 1898, courtesy of Southwest Museum.

Yunosi, a Havasupai woman in traditional late-nineteenth-century dress, with burden basket and milling stone at her feet. George Wharton James, ca. 1898, courtesy of Southwest Museum.

Waluthuma, known to Anglos as "Supai Charlie," ca. 1895. A nineteenth-century tribal leader, he was murdered by Anglos in Flagstaff after having been accused of cattle rustling but never brought to trial.

Havasupai schoolgirls playing stick game. Sticks were struck on the center stone so that they fell on the rebound; scores were noted on the circle markers. George Wharton James, ca. 1898, courtesy of Southwest Museum.

Havasupai women in front of wickiup with burden baskets and pitched water bottle. George Wharton James, ca. 1898, courtesy of Southwest Museum.

Rock Jones, shaman. George Wharton James, ca. 1898, courtesy of
Southwest Museum.

Paka-ga-kaba, a Havasupai elder, ca. 1898. Anglos, unable to pro-
nounce his name, called him "Package of Coffee." George Wharton
James, courtesy of the Southwest Museum.

Legends

The following twenty-six stories were collected from ten consultants by Carma Lee Smithson in the summer of 1958. Comments in parentheses are Smithson's; those in brackets are Euler's.

Although we do not have any other recordings of Havasupai myths and legends with which to make direct comparison, A. L. Kroeber's 1929 field party collected several from Walapai informants. Since I believe that the Walapai and Havasupai were one and the same ethnic group prior to 1880, when they were separated by government fiat, Kroeber's will serve excellently. Kroeber likened Walapai mythology to that of the lowland Yumans, especially the associations of Mountain Lion, Wolf, and Coyote, although he felt that the "cooperation-antithesis" of the two latter animals was Plateau-Shoshonean. Since *Walapai Ethnography* is now out of print, it will be of value to quote Kroeber's conclusions in their entirety:

> The Walapai are certainly not skillful story-tellers, even after allowance for imperfections and our rendering. Their motivations are crude and trivial; they do not consistently build up a character—except the essentially inconsistent Coyote; they do not always hold consistently to the hero even within one tale; and they do not seem to feel, or at any rate are unable to express, well-marked sympathy or identification with their personages, or to attach much emotion to them or their fate. They do like incident, irrespective of its inner connection with the plot; magic and trickery; and obscenity, sexual or otherwise.

The veracity of those statements is apparent in the Havasupai tales that follow.

Twelve of the legends in *Walapai Ethnography* are identical to those Smithson collected, varying only in minor detail and in certain geographical aspects that seem to be localized.

The Havasupai told these stories only during long winter evenings. If they were related during other seasons of the year it was believed that black widow spiders or snakes would bite the teller. Stories had no particular sequence. The storyteller or some-one in the audience would suggest favorites. Or the teller would ask for suggestions from the listeners. Some legends were specifi-cally designed for children, but none was withheld from them. Stories must be completed the same evening they are begun. If not, the teller or his listeners might become crippled in some way. Narrators of the tales usually were given presents of meat.

Origins

[This story contains certain elements of the usual Pai origin myths, but it also reveals data seemingly localized among the Havasupai bands.]

People [once] lived under the earth somewhere, nobody knows where, they lived underground where it was dark with no sun; they lived near a pool of water; there were just a few families liv-ing there.

One day two brothers, leaders, told their people what to do all the time. One of the men planted grape seed by the pool. The grapevine grew fast. It coiled around like a spider web, then shot out straight. Then people climbed up to the coil and stayed all night. Then they climbed to the next coil, stayed all night, and then up again. We don't know how many times they stayed all night; then they came on top of the ground.

Back at camp was a young lady who had stayed with all the men a few nights but none of the men wanted to marry her. She was jealous of other women. One day she was sitting beside the pool looking in the water when some women came with jars for water. One of the women said, "Why do you run off like this? We want you to come home." The woman grabbed her and started looking in her hair for lice. She saw many scars and asked what they were.

The young girl was mad and went down from the top and thought the men didn't like her. She wondered what she could turn into that men would like, so she turned into a tobacco plant growing beside the pool. The men gathered it and took it to the camp. They put it in the middle of their circle and started smoking it. Then the tobacco changed to a woman again and she said, "I thought you men didn't like me." She laughed and went off alone.

A few days later she was missed so a woman went to a spring. The woman looked for lice. The woman tried to grab her before she jumped into water to ask about her scars. She didn't answer, but turned into a frog and jumped into the pool. Then the water started to rise.

The men were sitting around talking. They thought the woman was all right. They were talking about this world. There was much small game, but they couldn't get close enough to see it in dark. So they asked their leader to make a light so they could see to shoot game. Older Brother said, "Yes, I can make a sun. But first you must go to bed and this will be night. Then someone must call, "It is daybreak, there will be a dawn in the east. The sun will come up and move across the sky to the west.'" So the people did as told. But at dawn it was the moon that came up. Older Brother said, "We'll call this Sun and we can see small game to kill it." But Younger Brother said, "No, that isn't bright enough. It looks shady and we can't see good enough." He said that it looks like an old man. He took a pipe wrapped around with sinew. He told them to go to bed as before and he would make a sun and call this one another name. At daybreak the sun came up and it was bright enough so they called the other one a moon.

At that time the sky was only half as high as now. The clouds passed by low and the sun went across too fast. Younger Brother took cane and pushed the sky higher so the sun and sky would be together.

Then people began to go around where they could see grass, springs, and other things in the world. They found plenty of game and thought this would be a good way to live.

At this time the frog-woman made the spring rise up through a hole to the first coil of the vine, then to the second, and on up to the top until it was covering the earth.

The people put a small girl in a log with the ends blocked
with pitch. She had with her food, water, birds, and animals. Two
men told her she would be going up and down in the water and
that they would all be drowned. She should remember the San
Francisco Peaks so she could find it if she came back to earth in
another place. She was to get water from a spring on top of the
peaks.

The water covered all the earth and drowned all the people.
It rose to the top of the sky so only a little woodpecker hung to the
top. He called, "*Gi-u Gi-yu.*" Water came up on his tail feathers
but he escaped. The water knew that the people were all drowned
so it receded. The flicker knew the log was still on the water and
followed it around. The log came to rest near *Ha²vuv²gwič*, a
waterfall on the Little Colorado River [Grand Falls]. The mountains near the falls are barren and there is no timber. This was the
first campsite the girl had. The mud was still soft, so she made
horses, grinding rocks, pots, and all things she could think of.
People say those things are still there. She got tired of staying in
the same place so she started out to find the mountain and spring
the two men had told her about. She found a spring dripping from
overhanging rocks and used the water to cook with.

She had grown up and was lonely, so she decided to make
another person. So in the early morning she lay down and spread
her legs so the sun's rays hit her vagina. Then she went back to
the waterfall and let water drip on her vagina. She became pregnant and had a baby girl. [In another version the girl was impreg-
nated by the flicker.] They lived together until her daughter was
grown. Then the mother told her daughter to do as she had done
to get a boy. The daughter did so and got a boy. He grew big
enough to hunt. He hunted many animals. The boy was the first
one to come to Supai. But the rock walls closed together to kill
people. Arrowweed grew here. People were always killed. The
boy was a fast runner so he jumped in, got some reeds, and ran
out fast before the rocks closed together. Then he returned to
camp.

He was the one who caught the eagle up high. He took an
animal hide and smeared it with blood. The eagle descended and
carried him off to its nest. He killed eight big ones in the nest and
four little ones; killed them all and took the feathers.

He prayed and blew his breath, and the rock wall turned to

sand so he walked down and took the feathers to camp so he
could make arrows with feathers to make them go straight.

He lived there for awhile with his grandmother and grandfather. One day he met a man. This was the dripping spring which
was his father. He had some horses and asked the boy which one
he wanted for his own. The boy chose a roan and the man said,
"That is my top horse. You break my heart but I have to give you
it." He had many saddles and told the boy to choose one. He
chose an old worn one. The man said, "You chose mine but I'll
have to give it to you."

Then he said, "Son, you must be like me." He lay the boy
on the ground and split him open and put lightning inside him.
He said, "I am the sun and the water and now you will be like me
forever. Come on and I'll show you the world." They visited a
tree that was in the sky and went many places.

The boy returned home and lived with his mother many
years. Then he thought it was no good to stay in one place all the
time. So his grandmother said, "I'll go west and take the big horses.
You go east and take the little horses. If you want to see me anytime, in the spring or fall, if the days are windy or cloudy, I'll know
you are coming to see me. I'll give you seeds. You can scatter them
along with the rain. You can say this will be grass, food, pinyons,
and other plants. There are many people in the world but they fight
one another but we will do this to keep them going.

The boy went to the east, his grandmother to the west. So
when the weather is windy and stormy we know the boy goes to
visit his grandmother.

Havasu Canyon Walls Closing Up

Version 1 Coyote said that long ago the walls of Havasu
Canyon used to close and open and close so no one could come
down this canyon. Many people were crushed between them. Then
two boys came down with arrows and tried to stop the walls from
closing. They shot arrows at the walls and this stopped them from
closing. So after that people could pass this way.

Version 2 Long ago these canyon walls moved back and
would close up and kill anyone who passed through here. This

happened repeatedly until many people were killed. Then a man
came and wondered how he would stop it. He carried a big log
on his head projecting on each side. The canyon walls closed but
were stopped by the log. They can't move any more, so from then
on people could pass through safely.

Version 3 It started from an old lady who lived somewhere
on the plateau. She had two boys. When they went around on the
plains up there they used to see much wild game, deer and rabbits. They wondered how to get them and kill them. Finally they
asked their mother and she told them to shoot them. "How
would we shoot them? With what?" She told them to use an
arrow. So they wanted to make arrows with feathers and points.
They asked where to get the reeds. She told them it was in a dangerous place and she didn't want them to go.

The reeds grew in the canyon at a place that was full of
bones. So they didn't tell their mother where they were going but
started out this way. They cut two long juniper trees; this kind
grows straight, as long as canyon is wide now. They started down
the canyon carrying the logs above their heads. When nearly to
the springs of Havasu Creek the walls closed up but were held by
the logs which wedged between them. So they came on down the
canyon and got the reeds. The logs were still wedged in the cracks
in old times, but have rotted out now. When the boys returned to
their mother she got after them and said, "I knew you were going
down there. That's why I didn't tell you the straight story. How
did you get through?" But they didn't tell her anything.

Frog Rock

[This story concerns a rock formation on top of the Redwall limestone near Supai village. It was narrated by two consultants.
Three others denied that any legend referred to the rock even
though the Havasupai generally refer to it as "Frog Rock."]

The frog came from the ocean on the west looking for a good
place to stay. He crossed the Colorado River below Needles, then
spent four more nights of jumping around, playing close to the
river. Then he took about a month more and he arrived in Hava-

supai Canyon. He was poised there ready to jump when he saw the river below. He was on the very edge of the rim when he turned to stone and could jump no more. Bagiova [a localized culture-hero] turned him to stone and made him stay right there for the Indians.

Origin of Menstruation

[Some portions of this are sung. Squirrel and his daughter had a mythical home in a canyon off the Topocoba trail about five miles from Supai village.]

Squirrel and his daughter and Coyote lived together. The squirrel was a little older than the coyote; he was the coyote's uncle. The squirrel went hunting and brought in a deer. While coyote was skinning it, he put his finger in the blood and flipped it on the inside of the girl's thigh. Coyote said to her, "Sister, you are menstruating. You can't eat the meat for four days." When he said that, the girl didn't believe him. Finally she grew angry; Coyote knew about menstruation but the girl didn't. She went to this side [north] of Seligman about ten miles where cattle tanks are now. She brought a spring forth there with the femur of a bobcat; people used to eat bobcat, that's why she had the bone. She split one piece of the bone lengthwise and put it on the ground. She left it a few minutes and pulled it out and water came forth. She traveled on to the southwest until she was thirsty again. Again she split a bone, put it in the ground, and brought water out. A spring is still there on the Walapai Reservation. [Perhaps Rose Well.] She kept doing this until she had made four springs, all the while traveling southwest. Then she reached some people camping at a village in the afternoon. An old lady was on the edge of the village. Some of the men were out hunting. When they returned, one shouted that there was a runaway girl and that she was going to be his. Another man said no, we'll look into it and see whose she will be. The men ate supper, and about dark they built a fire a little way from the house where the girl was staying with an old woman. The men started playing the sixteen-stick game. [A gambling game, wherein the sticks were used as counters. Probably borrowed from the Southern Paiute.] Every once in awhile a man would slip away from the game and go to the girl's house but she would beat them away and throw dirt on them. Even all the birds and animals tried, except the quail. Others told him to try but he said, "I'm not a good-looking man like some others she has turned down. So why should I try." But he finally tried. He put makeup on the feathers on his head and went in. She grabbed him and took him for her husband.

The men went hunting, all except the quail. He was lazy. Other men were jealous of him because he ate gravel and didn't hunt for meat. The men said they wouldn't give him any more meat.

Finally, the girl was expecting a baby. It was in the girl's thumb. When delivery time came, the girl went out and thrust her thumb in a forward motion and the baby stood up on the ground before her. After the baby boy was old enough, his mother wished for meat. She told him to go to Grandfather Squirrel who was a good hunter. The boy didn't say anything. After they went to bed, he got up, put a stick under his cover for a dummy, and went to his grandfather, the squirrel. The boy was approaching his grandfather's house when he came to some women picking pinyons. They gave some to him, and yucca juice to drink. When they set his food before him, he said, "This isn't good to eat, just good to soften leather of shoes." So he put it on his shoes. The juice was good for shampoo, so he washed his hair. Then he got his fine cornmeal lunch out and told them to eat. They said, "This isn't good to eat, just good for makeup." So they painted their faces with it. No one ate anything. Then they went to bed. The ladies were lying in a row. After they were asleep he got up and tied their hair together. In the morning he awoke and waited for the women to wake up. They slept on so he called out, "I never saw anyone sleep like that. I thought you wanted to work." One started to get up and all jerked each other, and laughed. Their hair was all tangled up. They saw he had a stone axe; he hit them on the back of their necks and killed them all. He beheaded them and hung them up in a tree. Then he took meat from their bodies and put it all in a sack. He went on to a village where the women's husbands were. He told them, "I saw many mountain sheep, rams, and killed them all. I left the meat in a bag a little way from here." Coyote was there, so he told Coyote to go and get the meat. He had left only half and brought the other half with him. They had a big pow-wow and everyone was eating the meat. Everyone then went to sleep. A vulture was a shaman and dreamed the truth. One man woke up and said, "The meat I was eating wasn't mountain sheep. Mountain sheep always melts in my mouth and this tastes different. I think it is human, lady's meat."

Vulture told Coyote to get the other half of the meat. He found it and decided to find the ram horns before he returned, so he followed the hunter's tracks and came to a string of black ants. He followed them to a tree and saw the human heads. He vomited, then went back and got the rope from the other half of the meat. He ran back to the village and yelled to people on the edge of town and told them to kill the boy. They hit at him repeatedly but couldn't get him. He said, "I never heard of people treating a visitor like this. I'll get away." So he [turning into a quail] flew up swiftly the way quails do, flew along, then down. The people tried to follow but lost him. He headed for his grandfather's village.

After he left his pursuers behind, he came to the place where his mother started from, on a point near Walapai Hilltop. He saw a deer running, almost winded, being chased by something. He shot the deer. Later he heard that Squirrel, his uncle, was the hunter.

After Quail Boy shot the deer, a dog went by so he shot him too. Old Squirrel came along and shouted out, "Who killed my pet? If you don't show up I'll make an earthquake, and you'll fall in where the ground splits apart." Squirrel kept repeating this so Quail Boy came out and said he was going to his grandfather. He said, "I had a grandfather living down that way and he told me to go to him and get some meat. I don't know why you act this way." Then the Squirrel was happy to see his grandson and embraced him. They made the dog come alive again, too. After they got acquainted, Squirrel put the dog on his instep and kicked him off toward the north, west, south, and east. He told the boy, "Be ready, for when the dog comes alive he may growl and come after you." He gave the boy the bladder from the inside of the deer to give to the dog so it wouldn't bite him. When kicked to the east, the dog came alive and the boy threw him the bladder when he growled. He ate the bladder and was friendly to the boy and came to him like a pet that had known him for a long time. After they got the venison, they returned to Squirrel's place, stayed together, hunted often. The coyote who lived with the squirrel went to another village and got killed. After they killed

Coyote, Quail Boy was angry and went to that village. After they missed Coyote, the grandfather, grandson, and dog went after the people. They sent the dog to the village to bite every person on the cords of their heels to cripple them. Then they came in and killed the people. They brought Coyote back to life as they had done with the dog and returned to their old home to live.

The Man Who Went After His Wife

A mother, her son, and his wife lived together on the Walapai Reservation about ten miles north of Rose Well, where foundations of their house can still be seen. [Several Cerbat branch sites, ancestral to the Pai, have been recorded in this vicinity.]

Earlier, when the boy was small, they lived alone. He had no father, but his mother took care of him until he became a good hunter. When he went hunting he would always return with meat. When he was old enough to marry, he thought he would cover more country to see if other people lived around. He would look for fire smoke or dust in canyons or mountains. He covered much area. Every morning toward the southwest he saw dust in the air, but it was far away. He asked his mother why she didn't tell the story about those people and why she had a home by herself for so long. His mother told him, "I just lived alone, long ago. I can't tell you we have friends or neighbors to visit. There are some people living far off in this world but they are enemies. I can't tell you to visit them as you might not return. We are doing well and getting along here as we are." But the boy had seen the smoke far off and when hunting had seen hunters' tracks where they chased deer. He was thinking strongly of getting married. (Here, the boy *sings* his part and his mother *speaks* in return.) He kept asking his mother where to go to see some people that weren't really animals, that wouldn't kill him, and who would talk to him as friends. [It was customary for the Pai to refer to all non-Pai in nonhuman terms.] His mother said, "No, if you go they will kill you. That's what happened here. We used to have many people, but all were killed and just two of us remain. We are doing all right as we are." The boy kept thinking of wanting a wife, and his mother finally said, "I know one place where you might find women gathering berries toward the east. They have good-looking women and built just right for men but they are hard to get. Many men go there to get wives, but their fathers usually kill the men. They are people called Bluebirds. You might find a wife there. They usually come out early in the morning and go home at noon. There are two sisters who work fast and finish their work first. Their husband is the blackbird, that follows around horses. Their father is the bluebird. They were birds but later turned into Hopi." The boy asked how to get there. His mother told him to cross the open desert, where he would first encounter a big herd of antelope in big open country: "When you see them you will know you are in the right country. Next you will see many rabbits in the brush; know you are going the right way. Next you will see many washes with mountain sheep. Know it is the right way. Next you will pass through wildcat country in cedars [junipers], one or two up in trees. Next you will run into a big herd of deer on a high ridge. Then you will come to lower country, an open valley with a big stream, but not deep, will cover your feet just to your ankles; the next river to cross will be up to your knees; the next will be above your waist, and the fourth will come up to your neck. You must cross four rivers and after that not far on is open desert and more level country. Stop, rest, look around; you may see women gathering grass seeds. That is where the two sisters come to find food." [Except for the reference to four rivers, this constitutes a fairly accurate description of the country along the Hopi-Havasupai trading trail.]

The boy said, "OK, I'll try to go that way and see if I can find those two ladies. You are all right, my mother, but you are getting old and can't get around like you used to. We need someone to keep house here."

His mother said, "OK, but be careful. There are many enemies in that country you must cross."

The boy started out, saw Red Butte and antelope herds running in front of him in the desert. He knew he was on the right way, and saw many rabbits. The boy said to himself in song, "If I want to make camp I'd shoot rabbits for food, but my mother's fire would die down so I must make this trip fast and return." So he went on, came through mountain sheep, then wildcats which he saw in nearly every tree; then he came to deer. Each time he saw things he made a song, saying, "I'm on my right way. Next will be the river up to my ankles." He came to it and ran on to the next river. He sang, "I'm on my right way. My mother was right." He came to the third river. Then the fourth. It was deep and he took his clothes off and bundled them on top of his head and crossed. He dressed and traveled a long distance farther. He saw a lone tree on the desert and went to it and rested under it. He looked around the country. Before long he began to smell like animals do, and soon caught scent of people. He thought they were nearby. When rested he started on and went over a high ridge. From there he could see many women moving in his direction. He watched and saw two sisters in front of the others. He thought they were the ones he was looking for. He made a plan as to what to do to ask the girls. He started downhill and ran close to them and stopped. They didn't look up, as they were gathering grass seeds, and came so close they nearly bumped into him. They stopped and looked up. Each one lay her burden basket in front of her and sat down bending over her basket. The boy sang to them to ask, if there was a visitor around, where is the house of a chief; "Don't be dying down without saying anything to me. I am looking for a wife. If you two are not married, I am ready to return from here to my mother's home. If you are married, I can't take you. I am dry and need water from your jug, if you have water."

One of the women reached in her basket and handed it to him without speaking or looking up at him. He drank and returned it. One of the girls said, "We are not married." He knew they were the ones married to Blackbird, but they said no to him.

He said, "OK, let's go back to my mother before her fire dies down. I can't leave one of you behind. Let's all hurry." They acted willing to go. They arose and left their burden baskets behind and followed him. They crossed the deep river, the next river, and the third; then one more to cross. It was late in the evening when they crossed the fourth river. They made camp that night. The next morning, he awoke and made song to them. He sang, "I thought you told me you were unmarried, but I dreamed your husband, a blackbird, was near our fire and made charcoal fly up, and I was in danger, but I have brought you this far."

They were still lying in bed, and right after he finished his song the blackbird caught up with them, flew to the fire, and knocked ashes over their fire. The blackbird asked the girls for something to take back with him. He kept asking them for things he really wanted.

The boy finally told the girls, "If a man has a wife he usually gives her clothing. Give the things back to him. I am ready to go on."

The older sister turned in her seat, and reached under her, and handed him something. He took it and left right away. This was a piece of flesh from inside a woman's body which is dangerous; if she pulls it out it will kill her like she was killed with lightning. Blackbird took it and put it on his head above his beak. That is the red feathers above his beak on that kind of bird. It has red on its wings.

The older sister acted like she was hurt bad; she couldn't travel fast enough to keep up and suddenly she dropped dead. The other two took her body, carried it to a pile of driftwood from the river, burned the body, then hurried on. They retraced their way to home.

Blackbird was a poor guy in those days. He didn't have things to make clothes for his wives.

The boy's mother was glad to see him home safe with a young lady. She was very glad to see them.

Before four nights were over, the mother asked the boy if it was all right to take the young lady to gather grass seed with her nearby. "I was doing it but am slow."

The boy said, "OK, but don't let her go as I brought her from a war place safely. If you let go of her hand, you will lose her."

His mother said, "I won't let her go. I'll gather seeds and shake them in the basket and return quickly." The boy said, "OK, but don't lose her, like I said."

The boy went hunting. In the evening his mother was home when she saw the boy returning. She said, "I did what you told me not to. I lost her not far from here. We were reaching for seed far apart on each side and I had to let go of her hand. In an instant she was gone. I don't know which way." His mother was half crying as she told it.

The boy said nothing till next morning. He asked his mother to show him the place. He went to the place, stood in his wife's footprints, blew snowy eagle down feathers toward the north, but it dropped; to the west, and it dropped; to the east, and it dropped. So he knew where she had gone. He blew feathers straight in the air above him; it had pull, and he went up in the air. His mother watched him ascending until he was out of sight. She began to cry and returned to camp.

The boy went up in the sky. There was a hole in the sky

where the wind went through to the top of the sky. He saw footprints of his wife and followed them to a village where he saw an
old lady in a doorway at the edge of the village. He said, "I'm the
one that lost a wife. If you saw her going this way I want you to
tell me where she was going and who was the man who took her."

The old woman said, "I didn't know it was your wife. It was
the wind. He is collecting wives and keeps them in his kiva in the
middle of the village. They are busy there every day."

The boy went on and saw the wind in person at the top
entrance to the kiva, tanning deerskin. He went up and asked him
if he had seen his wife. The wind said, "No, I don't know who is
your wife." But his wife had seen him and came over to the ladder and climbed up. But the wind kicked her stomach and
knocked her down the ladder. She tried again and he knocked her
down the ladder again.

The wind asked the boy to gamble with him, to put up his
hair as stakes. The boy said, "No, I don't want to play games. I
want my wife so I can take her home."

The wind said, "No, she belongs to me. You pull your
longest hair and if it is longer than mine you can have your wife."

The boy said, "My hair isn't long, but let's see yours." Wind
untied his hair and it hung only to his waist. Wind told the boy to
undo his. The boy untied his hair and let it fall down, but it only
unrolled partway, some still in the roll when it reached his waist.
The boy tied it up again and said to his wife, "Let's go home."

The wind said, "No, let's play another game." They played
many but the boy always won. The last one was a footrace. They
made lines and both walked to the line. Wind was fast but the
boy was faster. The boy thought first that the wind might be
faster, but he was slower. The boy outran him, so Wind turned
himself into a whirlwind and passed in front of him.

The boy said, "I don't want that kind of person to play with
me." Wind said, "OK, I'll just turn myself into a person."

So they played another game, and the boy planned to knock
on Wind's head with a rabbit stick.

They started to race again; the boy didn't try to run fast but
ran along beside Wind. Then Wind turned into a whirlwind, then
into a person again. The boy hit him with the stick and knocked
his head off. He returned and got his wife and they descended to
his mother's home.

He told his mother he was in danger now, so she must build a house four stories high with small holes around it. She said OK and started to build it. She made it solid. At the top was a smaller room with four small holes, one on each side so he could shoot in each direction.

The next morning after the building was finished, early in the morning when they were asleep, thunder came that shook the house. Next, swarms of small birds came from the sky and tried to shoot the boy. But he hollered a war cry and shot every direction from the top room all day. It rained all day, but near evening the clouds began to break up. They slept that night inside.

The next morning the same things happened: thunder, birds, and he shot at them all day and killed most of them. The third day, the same. The fourth day, the same. In the evening the boy was tired; his hands were sore. He couldn't pull the bowstring any longer. So he made a plan. "These people won't stop coming every day. I'll make a plan to run away to the south where the sky is closer." At night they left the house and traveled to the south. Near morning his mother was very tired. The young man thought if they traveled days through the country the people would follow and kill them all. So he told his mother they would leave her there. She lay on her stomach and he covered her with ice lumps and told her to watch the sky for a string they would lower. He and his wife went on and by daybreak they reached a place where sky and earth meet, and climbed over the place to where his mother was, and lowered the string to her. She grabbed it and tied it around her waist. The boy and his wife both pulled and lifted her up to the top of the sky. Most of the Sky People are living up there so they wanted to turn into Sky People. They have wings and they have no trouble with those people there, but every morning they could hear thunder below at their old home and see rain until the attackers learned that they had left the stone tower.

Every time the young man spoke, it was song. Others, Mother, Wife, Blackbird, and Wind do not sing. Every time he spoke he sang.

(On his journey to get a wife, it is in song; also the return journey is in song.) [It could not be ascertained with certainty whether this was to be sung in the first or third person.]

(The consultant learned this story from his maternal

grandfather and great uncle, Panamida, who was his mother's father's younger brother. His great uncle told it until his death about 1943. The consultant thinks he may have omitted some detail.)

The Lady Who Could Have No Children

A man and his wife lived together at a place. She could not have children. In the fall when it was clouding up, a south wind was blowing hard against their house.

The wife said, "Why don't you get busy and stop up the holes in our house? The weather is getting colder. The wind is blowing away most of what I grind."

The man said, "All right, I'll try to fix the house and get some wood in so we can stay in this room all winter."

He began with the house to fix it, on a windy, cold day. Every time he came with logs to fix it, he put them around like a hogan. Every time he brought a pole as he went back, his wife was grinding grass food [seed]. By doing that she would be ready for the next meal. The man came to the grinding rock and reached down and took some food and put it in his mouth. He kept eating what she was grinding each time he passed by with a pole. After awhile, the wife, when he reached for it, pushed his hand away half mad or trying to make trouble. She said, "I don't want you to take any more. I'm tired and want to get enough for our meal but you keep eating by yourself."

Then she said, "You're not acting as a man's way. We shouldn't have to stay here, as your parents died just a little way from here. We used to have a village here, but all are killed. But you don't do anything to your enemies. When I say this it will make you mad."

The man kept getting poles, pretending he didn't care about what she said. After the house was repaired, he brought firewood. Later, during the night, he thought over by song what she had said. "Why did you say those bad things to me? If you wanted me to do something, why didn't you say it when the trouble was fresh, when the tracks were fresh. It looks like you want to get rid of me. What are you trying to get at? Tell me what you really mean, and I'll think it over."

The next day she said, "I didn't mean anything. I was just mad because you kept getting that food I was grinding. I didn't mean anything."

The next day he sang again, "I was trying to fix the house and eat a little of your grinding. Maybe you wanted me to fix a good house and do hard work. Maybe you wanted a house of your own and live by yourself here. What are you driving at? If I leave you alone and go to war do you think you can live by yourself here and go hunting and do hard work? I think it's hard for a woman to live by yourself."

His wife replied, "I don't want you to feel bad over what I said. Just forget that. We live here by ourselves and it is good."

The next day after she pushed his hand away, she cooked and told him to eat. But he said, "No, I can't eat your food. You pushed my hand away." She cooked more, but he refused to eat. He went around and ate his own food. Four days later the man said to the lady, "Lady, I'm trying to be on war. From today on I'll fix me a suit of clothes, buckskin moccasins and leggings and pants." Each thing took one day [including a] coat and headdress. He took arrowweed. He fixed a reed to drink water from a deep water hole. Then he asked his wife to go along and show him the place where they had the big fight.

She said, "No, I don't think it's fair. I don't want to go. I said that one thing, but you just kept it up. Now you've got ready to fight." The man said, "If you don't show me I'll kill you. You are asking for trouble."

So the lady took him there just a little ways and showed him the village, rotten timbers of houses and the fighting ground nearby. They returned to their home. Next morning, the man said to the lady by song, "I'm going just over the ridge and stay there till next morning. I'm ready for this fight and want to see if you think I'm powerful. I'm going to practice on you."

The lady thought she was going to live there alone, and got scared, but answered the man.

The next evening he took his new clothes and said, "When I come out from the top of the ridge, and you watch me coming down from top, I'll holler '*Ba²ha²o*' (danger). You repeat my words."

He went over the ridge and they did this. He called the word. She repeated it. She and the house all flew up in the air, scattered, and came down. She fell unconscious, then came back alive. She said, "I didn't know you were that kind of man. I believe that what happened when you hollered that second time. It sounded like your voice was many and I didn't know what happened next. I believe you are powerful."

The next day he sang, "This is the day I am planning to leave you. I don't know whether my plan will work out. You watch over that high ridge. If I'm alive I'll stand on that ridge."

He started out, went to the scene of the battle, and looked for signs of which direction the enemies had gone. He took south and started out. Before too late in the evening he came to some old camp fires and places where trees were chopped down. He hunted for rocks used for pillows when men wanted to sleep lightly. He saw rocks used by the leaders, counted them, and figured out this must be that chief. He thought which one belonged to which bird. He thought he must stay overnight and use their pillows. Before daybreak he went on. He traveled day after day till he came to a camp where the brush was fresh. They had stayed awhile at each camp to hunt. He was traveling on every day so he knew he would overtake them. He began to skip a camp and go on to the second one before sleeping. He would use the same pillows. By doing that he finally saw the place where they had just left that morning. The fires had hot ashes and smoking charcoal. He thought he could overtake them the next day. So he stopped and used each pillow, changing from one to another through the night to get their thinking in his mind. So when fighting he could witch them to kill them. He had changed from one pillow to another through each night of the trip. That was the reason he had stayed in their camps.

In song he said, "This is the pillow of 'so-and-so'. He thinks he is a powerful man to be chief. I got his thoughts from his pillow."

In song he also thought of his wife, "She thinks I can't go to these people and act as a man. When I come close she thinks I'll be a coward and just throw rocks or sticks. That is the way ladies fight, talk a lot and throw rocks or sticks. I don't want to fight like a lady. I want to act like a man. I'll show her the heads and faces so she will say I am a man fighter."

When he came to an encampment, he made a ring around it by night. While changing pillows he caused the ring to build up by praying, hard, shiny, high. This was his fighting ground inside. It was far enough from the village that people couldn't see it.

That morning he said, "This is the day to fight. I'm not alone. I have help with me but no one knows. If I win the fight this morning I can gather the chiefs' heads in a bundle and take them home. I'm going to have a man fight. I won't sneak up while they sleep. I'll get close and listen if any chief talks to people, and I'll know they are all up and ready to hunt."

A chief spoke, "We aren't going to live at this place but will move on as those two back there may still come after us. We'll go out and hunt today for food. Then we'll move on to another camp as we have been doing."

He knew they were afraid and started running toward them while the chief was talking. When he came into camp some men were up and some had eaten; some saw him coming and said, "A visitor is coming." The chief looked and said, "That's not a visitor, it's an enemy on the warpath."

They gathered their weapons and got into one place. He watched them. When they were ready they called, "*Ba²ha²o.*" He called, "*Ba²ha²o!*" and ran to their camp, and all the people flew up in the air, and came down. He ran to them, ran around hitting all in their heads; he cut all the chiefs' heads off, but left women and children as they were, but collected chiefs' heads.

He sang, "I'm not going to stay here. I'm going to run back this day and show my wife these heads. In my early life I used to run around the world twice each morning."

He started running back and came to a ridge. He put the heads together on a long stock and hung it in a little tree. He ran to the ridge top and hollered to the lady so she would look. He ran on without carrying anything with him.

The lady said, "What's the matter? They usually come back with the heads of chiefs. You don't have anything, just alone. Why?"

The man said, "Look at my clothes and my hands. Does it look like I've been in a fight, or got scared and ran back from those people?"

She felt bad at him.

He said, "All right, you saw me standing back there. Run over there and see if you find anything. Get the heads and bring them. Make a round dance because I'm the winner. If you don't see anything they are the winner."

She did as told and made a round dance.

Next morning he told the lady to run over the ridge where the sun rises. "Get a yucca plant and bring it back so I can take a bath. I'm bloody and dirty from my trip. I should be clean before I take my first meal at the house."

Before sunrise she brought the yucca and gave him a bath and a shampoo and painted his body red all over. After his body and hair dried up they boiled meat and other food; when his hair was really dry, they ate together. From that he said that when anybody fights in this world, they must wait until their hair dries before eating. If they don't they will get gray young.

After they did this they both went up in the air and made themselves Sky People. They live up there and have wings.

Grandmother and Little Boy

(This story begins, "When animals were like humans, the grand-mother, her two sons, the two girls, and her grandson were all humans; the others were animals." The story is narrated in song and text. All the songs are sung by the mother of the two boys and the grandson. Neither the boys nor the girls sing.)

Two boys and their mother who was in mid-age lived in camp on the plains [plateau]. The boys were small and didn't know how to hunt wild rabbits and bigger game. They started shooting small birds that came near their houses, until they were big enough to try bigger game. They used a stick to flip a pebble at birds. When they were old enough to go farther from home, their mother didn't tell them where to go to get arrows. But they had been on the rims of Cataract Canyon and saw arrowreeds down here; they saw the canyon walls closing together. They returned to their mother and asked her where to get arrowreeds. Their mother said, "There is no place around here to get arrowreeds." But they had already seen this place. Their mother didn't want to tell her boys as it was too dangerous. [See "Havasu Canyon Walls Closing Up" on page 39 for other versions.]

A few days later their mother went to get hardwood that grows on the foothills of mountains like Bill Williams. She cut good-size timbers, one for each to carry on his head. Whenever the canyon walls moved together the logs would stop the walls. They went ahead without telling their mother. They started slowly down the canyon to see if the logs would hold the walls, and saw that they would hold steady. The walls were held apart by the poles, so the boys untied them from their heads and went on down the canyon across from where Lee and his family live now to gather arrowreeds. They selected the best ones and went home. As they approached they said, "We must hide these and go to our mother and ask if she has things for our arrows." They asked her, "If we gather those arrowreeds, would you mind straightening out the shafts for us?" She almost hollered, "Those walls almost always kill people who go there. It takes a fast runner to get a few and get away alive."

One of the boys returned to the cache and brought arrowreeds to his mother. She was excited that they had gone. They told her how they had done it. The mother said to them, "All right, put it away, boys. I'll try to straighten those arrows by morning. You'll have to go some distance away from the house to play and don't hide nearby to watch. If you do, the arrows will break and not be strong." They asked how she would straighten the crooked ones, but she didn't want to tell them.

Next morning she sent them away. The boys wondered about how she would do it, so they talked it over and decided to return and peek through the door. When they came near the door one stood almost and watched.

He saw his mother sitting with her legs apart, working the arrow back and forth in her vagina to straighten it, then hold it up and sight along to see if it was straight. Then it broke and his mother looked and saw the boys. She called out, "Why are you watching me? I'm going to spank you both." She ran after them, but they ran away and were afraid to return. That evening they returned, approaching cautiously, and looked in. Their mother said nothing, so they went inside. They saw the reeds all straightened standing against the wall. They didn't know what to do for points. So their mother said, "There is a place where you can get hardwood to make arrow points, but it is owned by Owl, and he is too selfish to let anyone have it."

The boys wondered what they could do to get hardwood. The boys went to the place and made a noise to attract Owl's attention. Owl heard them and answered. Boys said, "We didn't come to have trouble with you. Our mother sent us to ask you to come live with us and become her husband." Owl said, "OK, you get what hardwood you want and pack it to carry to your home."

That evening the mother saw them returning, and Owl was with them. She called out, "What are you doing? I don't want you to be around Owl." The boys said, "We want you to be good to him. He let us have this wood for our arrow points. We want him to live with us." The Mother said, "All right." Owl lived with them as their father. A few days later Owl and the boys went hunting together. They got game and cut the large intestine out and tied it at both ends. The plan was to put his eyes out. They told Owl to watch it. They put it on the fire to cook. They told him they always prepared food like that. It expanded with heat, exploded, and charcoal flew up and put his eyes out, and they killed him.

Then the boys wanted rock for arrow points. Their mother said, "Bear owns that and it is dangerous." The boys made a plan. They went to Bear and invited him to return and marry their mother. Bear said, "OK, you get what rock you want and pack it to carry to your home."

That evening the mother saw them returning and Bear was with them. She called out, "What are you doing? I don't want you to be around Bear." The boys said, "We want you to be good to him. He let us have this rock for our arrow points. We want him to live with us." The Mother said, "All right." Bear lived with them as their father.

Bear stayed at home while the boys went hunting. They figured a way to kill Bear. One of the boys started to put hardwood at the end of an arrow. He split an end to see if Bear would laugh at them. The boy took charcoal from the fire, worked it with his finger and made an arrow point. Bear laughed and said, "I don't think you will kill much with that soft thing." The boy said, "All right. I'll show you when I finish this." He made it and told Bear to walk some distance away and hold his arms up above his head. "We'll see if it bumps off your skin." Bear said, "All right." Bear walked over there—while he was going over there, the boy took the charcoal point away, threw it aside, and took a stone point from a hiding place in his clothing, and quickly wrapped it on the shaft with string. Bear turned and said, "Is this as far as you want me?" Boy said, "Farther, like I was shooting at deer." Bear walked

on and the boy called, "Right there." The boy pulled the bowstring tight. Bear, when he thought the boy was ready to shoot,
jumped aside a little. The boy said, "Hold still." Bear said, "I'm
not moving. It's just the wind moving. My hair makes it look like
I'm moving." The boy let the arrow fly, and it hit Bear under his
arm and through the body and out the other side on the ground.
Bear ran toward the boys but fell dead before he reached them.

A few days later, the boys asked their mother where would
be a good place to find feathers. Arrows were made without
feathers until that time. Their mother said, "I don't think there is
a good place for you to get feathers." They kept asking, but she
wouldn't tell them. The boys had already seen an eagle's nest in a
hole in a cliff. Their mother said no, but the boys made ready to
go. They took deer hide, wet it, and stretched it over their bodies
and let it dry hard in the shape of their bodies. The boys had it
fixed to lace strings across their stomachs to hold the hide like a
hard shell on their backs, so they could lie flat, and the eagle
claws would strike the hide.

They started out and heard the sound of an eagle. They
went a little farther in their armor hides so the eagle would break
it, and the blood would make him think he had killed something.
When the eagle swooped on them, they lay down. The eagle drew
blood, and carried them off to his nest where two small eagles
were. He said, "It's bleeding," and told the young to eat it. The
old eagle flew a little distance away and sat watching.

The boys sat up, and the young called to the eagle, "This
thing is still alive," but Old Eagle didn't look back. The boys
asked Young Eagles not to tell Old Eagle, so they kept still. The
boys had two (or a few) throwing sticks like Hopis use for rabbits. One stood up, threw it at Old Eagle and hit his neck and
knocked him down to the bottom of the cliff.

The boys asked the young eagles how many old eagles lived
there. Young Eagles said about eight. The boys told them not to
tell so they wouldn't have to kill them. Old Eagle returned and
asked Young Eagles, "What was that noise? I thought I heard you
two young fall to the bottom." Young Eagles said, "We didn't
hear any noise. We don't know." Old Eagle flew over to the place
the first one had sat and looked the other way. The boy threw a
stick and killed him. He repeated until three were killed. He said,
"I have killed three, must wait for five more." Then he repeated

all this until all eight were dead. The boys then took the two young eagles, swung their heads around, and threw them to the bottom. The boys stood there and prayed for the high cliff to sink to the ground so they could walk down. The cliff sank until just a little hill was left. The boys walked home.

Their mother said, "How did you manage this? Even the best hunters don't know how to do it." The boys said, "We just learned how to manage things from you, my mother."

They had plenty of feathers to make arrows. The boys hunted and got much meat. They would kill big bucks and pack them home. They had lots of meat.

The mother told the boys not to think about ladies for their wives. Later on, two ladies from far to the south came. The two boys climbed up on a roof to sleep and always made music before sleeping. The girls, far to the south, heard the music and decided to find out what it was. They traveled north day by day toward the music. Before they got there, they saw a lizard and asked what that noise was. Lizard said, "I'm the one that makes music every night. But now I'm cooking my meal here." The girls said, "OK, eat, and then we'll hear your music." Lizard ate and then reached to one side of his house and got red paint and painted under his eyes and on his face to make himself pretty. He told them to listen. He went a little way and climbed on a rock. He lay on his belly and swelled his belly and breathed hard.

He said, "I'm the one that's doing this. Is this what you heard?" The girls said, "No, that isn't it." Then they heard the boys making music not far away. They played on an instrument made from jointed sticks. It is hollow and grows on Bill Williams Mountain. It's not a grass, but is called "music bush." *Tal²tal* is the name of the instrument. I don't know how it was made, maybe like a flute.

The girls said, "We like that music." They thought to themselves, "We want to climb up there and sleep with those boys when it gets dark." The mother knew what they wanted and sat in the doorway and sang a song. She said, "The girls are made out of blood and something else. They came from the west where it is dark night. They are no good for you. You already know how to kill wild game. They will spoil your luck."

The mother sang this and later on reached over and got dried meat and fat from what the boys had hunted. The girls held it in their hands and waited for the old lady to go to sleep. The mother sat there, talked to the boys, told them not to take a chance on the girls. The girls thought it would soon be morning and wanted to find a way to make the old lady sleep. The younger girl had some medicine. She poured it on the old lady, and she went to sleep. They jumped over her and climbed up where the boys were.

The older boy didn't want them and rolled up tight in his blanket. The girls had a hard time, but before morning the younger boy loosened his blanket and let a girl crawl in with him. So the girls decided to leave before the mother awoke. The girls left and went some distance away. The older sister said, "Let's stop and urinate and see which one finishes first. If I finish first you must leave me here and go home alone." The older sister had a hard time getting through, but Younger Sister finished right away. Older Sister wanted to leave Younger Sister there; she said, "You are already married." She tried to leave her there, but she ran along after Older Sister until they were home.

The boys went hunting and Younger Brother got two small deer. Older Brother got two big bucks. They carried them home. Their mother said, "I told you girls were bad luck. That's what you get for not listening to me."

A few days later, the mother asked Younger Brother to gather yucca; to bring the plant to her, wash with it, run east and back to the house, to recover his hunting luck.

He did this and his luck was better. He went hunting several days. Then they made plans to see the girlfriends at their homes. They told their mother to stay at home. They each pulled one of the longest hairs from their heads and tied them in the room stretched from one wall to the other. They told their mother while they go away to the girls if anything happens, if they get killed while away, the two hairs will break and bleed.

They went on the trip to the girls' home. Their mother kept her eye on the hairs. Finally it broke in half and bled on the ground. The mother began to cry and wished to be dead the same as the boys.

The boys reached the home of the girls. Younger Sister had a baby almost ready to be born. One of the sisters ran to the place where a big hawk lived and said, "Two cottonwoods have come into our home," and asked him to kill them both. The hawk flew down and cut their heads off in two swoops and returned home.

(The boys were human in the story. Then the hawk flew down over their heads and knocked one down, butting his throat as he passed by. It flew up, turned, and killed the other one, and flew off to its home in the cliff. After that the boys were called two cottonwoods.)

Later on, Younger Sister had a baby boy. She kept him there; he grew fast and watched men play games. The sisters told the boy to "come back home or they'll get you with those bones. Your father was killed here and we fed you all this time in his skull made into a bowl."

The boy felt bad and thought of the troubles they had before he was born. He didn't want to eat from his mother. He climbed on the roof and cried. His tears ran down the support poles like on a brush shelter. He heard that men were going the next morning on a rabbit drive. He waited until the men were gone, climbed down, and asked his aunt where the big hawk lived. His aunt said, "You mustn't go over there. It is on a high cliff; he has a hole in middle of the cliff. You can't get up there." The boy said, "I want to see it." His aunt pointed out the place.

The boy started for it, walked faster, and ran. The boy stood below and saw the hawk sitting on the edge of the hole. The boy blew his breath toward the hawk. He had an eagle feather, so he blew it up in the air and followed it up through the air. He climbed up behind the hawk and said, "I want some of that wood to hunt rabbits with." The hawk looked back and said, "How did you get up here? No one can climb up here." The boy said, "I'm in a hurry. I need that wood." The hawk was tanning deer hide and he said, "There is some in the house. Reach up and get it from on top." The boy reached under a pile and found the two bloody pieces that had killed his father and uncle. He made several swings toward Hawk and then let fly before he looked back and killed Hawk.

The boy blew against the cliff. It turned to a sandy place so he walked down.

The boy hurried to the place where the hunters were with the wooden things from Hawk's house. He said to the men, "Better stand together at one side. This wood won't go straight. I want to throw it."

The men said, "Is this OK?" He told them to stand closer together. He swung it a few times, then let go. It flew to the men and hit around their necks so they were all killed.

He took a wooden stick. He ran fast toward home and killed his mother, aunt, and all the other women. He stood around alone. It looked like his aunt was coming alive. She moved once in awhile. He sang to her and said he wished her to come alive so he could ask her which direction his father came from. The aunt finally quit moving and died. So he took his own direction, traveling and looking around for his grandmother. He finally happened onto her living alone. But she was all dirty from where she had rolled in a fire and falling off a cliff to kill herself. She had finally given up trying suicide and sat around there.

The boy stood awhile. His grandmother said, "I'm not fit for a young boy like you. Go away, don't come near me. I'm by myself." The boy said, "I thought you were my grandmother. My father and mother are dead. They say you are my father's mother. I wanted to see you."

She embraced him and cried awhile. When she stopped, she said, "My grandson, I feel a little better since you say you are my grandson. I can't move from here because my sons' things are here and I'm watching their things."

Then the grandmother and the little boy lived together. When he was big enough to hunt, he did as his father had done. He made a lovely home and brought much meat home.

When the boy was in middle age, his grandmother said to him, "I have a plan for us to split here. My grandson, you take all the horses and the best things your father had and move toward the east. Leave me here. I'll take our heavy horses and old things and I'll move toward the west. This is the place where your father hunted when he was alive, so I don't want to be here anymore. We won't die, we'll live forever. When you wish to visit me, you must travel across the sky with the clouds. You can carry seeds of different kinds: grass food, pinyon nuts, and cedar berries each time, and drop them on the ground—sow it from the air—as you travel. You must visit me but I can't visit you." [See "Origins" above for another version.]

So they did that. The grandmother lives near a big ocean and is still alive. She wasn't a bird, she was human.

The Sun and His Daughters

[Sunset Crater National Monument, the vivid cinder cone of a volcano that erupted in the eleventh century A.D., is located several miles northeast of Flagstaff, Arizona, on the southeastern edge of the former, aboriginal range of the Havasupai.]

The sun used to live at Sunset Crater, its home. Tribes used to gather around Sun's home and play games. Tribes played with Sun; Sun was the hero and always won. They played the sixteen-stick game. The tribes kept betting a little bit of hair on their bodies at a time until they lost all their bodies. Sun used them for meat. He made prickly pear cactus red fruit from the blood of animals. He used tears for drinking water. He took the liquid from inside the eyeball and made corn from it. He made beans from the kidney. He used this method to get food to feed men when the tribes gathered to play games. He gets the guts and makes dried pumpkin. He took meat from people and made deer meat from it. He fed them this food, called different tribes to games, and beat them until he killed all the tribes but one from the north rim [of Grand Canyon], the lion. The ground was higher on the north rim, and he looked toward Flagstaff. The lion could see smoke from a fire built by Coyote, who built a fire in the brush they lived under. Then Coyote could get them and eat them (muskrats, ground squirrels, small ground animals about the size of a mouse). The lion kept watching, and went across the canyon to see what Coyote was eating. He crossed on this side of Red Lake. [Near the present Williams, Arizona–Grand Canyon highway.] A large village was there. He went to house after house but all were empty. He found no human being, just one old coyote. The lion approached him by sneaking up to see what Coyote was doing. The lion watched from outside. Coyote lay inside a house like he was starving, snapping at the flies that came around on his face. The lion asked where everyone was. Coyote said, "There is no one here but me. I built all this village myself and am alone here." Lion said, "This can't be true because I have seen (feces) from babies wrapped up in the trees." Coyote said, "No, this is all from me, all my (feces)." Lion knew Coyote was lying and asked Coyote to tell him the truth, but Coyote kept insisting he was the only one around and no other people lived there. The lion said, "Well, if you said you are by yourself, give me some food to eat." Coyote said, "I am hungry. I've got nothing to eat. I'm starving." The lion said, "You've been making fun of me. I want you to go fetch the meat I dropped just before I reached the village." The coyote said he was glad to go get it. He went but couldn't lift the meat; it was too heavy. It was wrapped up in a deer hide. So the lion went back and brought it to the house and they cooked it. After eating they bedded down. Before daybreak Lion said, "I want to ask you again. You have been kidding me. I want to know where the people went."

The coyote didn't speak for awhile, then said, "I'll tell you the right story. There used to be many people here. Then the sun killed them one after another when they gambled with him and lost, until they were all dead. I am the only one left." After Coyote told the truth, the lion said, "That is what I wanted you to tell me so I would know what to do." The lion told Coyote to make all different sizes of flint arrowheads, a whole pile of them, bundle them in deer hide and put them to the east; then before dawn, take the whole skin of flints and throw it toward the sun. "Be sure not to leave any little pieces lying around but have every one inside the deer hide and throw them all." Coyote did it and returned. The lion said, "This wasn't done in vain. This isn't the end. The things you threw out will come to life and return to the village. I am telling you ahead of time. You must go into your house and not peep out or do anything foolish no matter if you hear people chopping wood or whatever you hear. Stay inside until evening." Lion told Coyote these things. Then the sun rose and they soon heard people's voices in the village, but Lion heard only old people, no small children, and he knew Coyote hadn't obeyed. The coyote pretended he knew nothing that Lion had told him and said, "Uncle, I hear people's voices and I want to peep outside." Coyote tried to beat the lion outside but the lion grabbed him and said, "My head itches. It must be some kind of bug in my hair. I want you to see what it is." He held Coyote there. Finally evening came. Both went out and peeped into house after house but saw only old people. The lion said, "You didn't obey me. What did you do with the small chips?" Coyote said, "I threw the big ones toward the sun and the small ones just behind me." Lion said, "That is all right as long as we got everyone back but we don't have any little children. Tonight we'll have a meeting because if we keep looking at him [the sun] he will keep on killing men until there won't be a living creature around here." After this talk they decided to meet after sunup. The lion said, "I'm not the smart one, but I know one who is: the squirrel. He is the smart fellow. He lives at Rain Tank south of Tusayan [near Grand Canyon village on the south rim]. The lion said, "He thinks real good. He'll know what to do and we can ask him." After they held the meeting, and everyone agreed to a plan, the lion sent Coyote after Squirrel. The lion told Coyote to tell the whole story with eloquence and tell him the sun would kill everyone if they didn't get help. So Coyote started off. There were two [squirrel] brothers living at Rain Tank. The oldest one lay on top of pine trees and watched, and the younger one was inside a tree. The older one saw smoke signals of Coyote approaching and said, "Somone is coming, Younger Brother. I want you to put some meat on the fire to feed whoever is coming. It looks like it is coming toward our place." The younger one said, "Coyote always makes smoke when he burns out small animals around those peaks where he lives. I don't think he is coming here." "Yes, he is getting near and is really coming to our camp." The younger brother said, "It must be somone to tell us bad news; there must be trouble somewhere." The older one said, "They must have been attacked by another tribe somewhere. They have come for help. I can see the man now. It looks like Coyote."

When Coyote reached the house he didn't speak. The brothers were smart and didn't want to ask; they wanted him to tell of his own accord. They gave him food. He ate and pretended he was on his own business. They slept and Coyote didn't say anything. Older Brother got after Coyote and said, "All you want to do is eat. When I saw smoke signals approaching I knew it was to tell of trouble and ask for help. They call out before they reach the house and tell their trouble that someone attacked them or otherwise. But you didn't say even a word. You just eat."

Coyote said, "Yes, I was on a mission to tell of trouble." Then Coyote recounted the entire story that had gone before: "The lion told me to come here and ask your help but I didn't say it out." After Coyote told the story they said, "OK, we'll help but won't start today. We'll start tomorrow." He told Younger Brother to tie hides in the trees and to bury some of their things to prepare to leave their camp.

Next day they started back to the village and reached it. The lion told them the whole story. The two brothers said, "Yes, it is a sad story. The sun is a real smart man and no one can ever beat him. He will keep on until he kills everyone. It is good that you told us your story. Now we'll try to do something about it. We'll ask the badger to help. If we went on top of the ground the sun would see us and kill us. The badger says he is a good digger so we'll ask him to dig a tunnel to the sun's house and under the house where the sun has hides of men on the floor, and all people would go into the tunnel and into the house." After Badger did it, the older brother inspected and found it went zig-zag and never reached the sun's house. So he called Prairie Dog to try and dig a straight tunnel to the sun's house. "You say you are a good digger. Now let's see if you can do it!" The prairie dog said, "OK," and started from where he was sitting; but before he went far he came up to the top. The two brothers inspected and found it wasn't good; it kept coming to the top of the ground, instead of staying underground. They called the ground squirrel, who said, "OK, I'm a good digger." He did better than the others but went straight, then down, then zig-zag, then up. The brothers inspected and said, "No, it isn't right."

Then they called for the pocket gopher, the kind Coyote used to eat. He was the best digger and went straight to Sun's house. They told him to feel the man's hide on Sun's floor and leave it there. They inspected and said it was right. Then they went back and told people it was what they wanted. They came out of the tunnel and told the people it was time to start. They said, "We'll go through the tunnel; Sun will hear us but we'll keep going until we come into the sun's house. We'll line up along the wall. We'll be the leaders with Lion next to us and will stand along the wall and wait to see what Sun will do." They followed the plan and Sun heard a rumble as people walked through the tunnel. He was on top of his house. He looked around but could see no one. So he went into his house. The two brothers were in the middle and the others were along the walls. Sun shone full on them trying to blind them but they didn't blink. Finally, Sun got tired and said, "I thought you were children but you are not." So Sun gave up. Sun got an elk antler and threw it in front of them. He told them to split it in two (like a sling shot). This was a game he had always used to beat men. The brothers said, "We never heard of this. Visitors should always be given food and drink and not asked to play games so the host can beat them. You want us to break this and it isn't even hard." Older Brother picked up the antler and easily broke it apart and into small pieces and threw it

on the floor before Sun. After this, Sun called his daughters. He
asked them to bring water for the visitors. The girls brought a
pottery jar of water and set it in the room and watched. Coyote
got excited and spoke up, "I'm thirsty and want to drink." But
the brothers told him to sit down. "How do you know it is
water? If it is real water it should have green willows in the
mouth of the jar." This was in a bowl instead of a proper pottery
jar with a small mouth closed by a lid of willows from the spring
to keep water from slopping out. Older Brother told Coyote that
it wasn't water. He told Coyote to throw it out. He said, "I
thought it was real water and I used to drink it. Maybe I have a
bad odor so he doesn't want to kill me."

The sun asked his daughters to grind cornmeal and make
mush for the people. When the corn mush was cooked and set
before the people, no one wanted it except the Coyote as before.
Older Brother said, "It isn't corn. We saw no cornfields and no
cornhusks lying around. They made the corn out of the fluid of
the eyes of humans." He told Coyote to throw the corn mush out,
so he did.

Next the sun called his daughters to cook meat and soup for
the people. They did. When served to the people Coyote was the
only one who said he was hungry. He said he was going to drink
the soup. Older Brother said, "If this was real meat it would have
some hair on it like deer meat. This meat came from your body so
if you eat it the sun will win again. I want you to throw it out."
So Coyote did as he was told.

Next Sun told his daughters to cook beans for the people
and they were served to people on the floor. Coyote said, "I'm
wishing for beans and want to eat." Coyote started toward it. But
Older Brother said, "This isn't real beans. You should have seen
farms. I saw no leaves around here. Throw it out or he'll beat you
on this." So Coyote did.

Sun called his daughters to cook prickly pear fruit to drink.
They fixed it in pottery jars. Coyote jumped up and said, "I used
to wish for this kind." Older Brother said, "This is made of your
blood." So Coyote threw it out.

All these things were made from the bodies of victims. Sun
called for his daughters to cook pumpkin. Coyote repeated his
wishes but Older Brother said, "If this was real pumpkin you
would see fields and leaves; it is made of your guts. They will beat

you." Coyote said, "Why is the sun trying to trick us on this? I thought it was real." He threw it out.

The sun told his daughters to bathe and wash themselves with sand and to sharpen the teeth inside their vaginas and to lie down in a row without clothes on. The visitors came and circled around where they were lying. Coyote spoke first and said he wanted to have intercourse first. "This is just what I've been wanting to do." Squirrel said, "No, don't. I'll be the first. I'm the oldest. See what happens first. They have teeth in their vaginas and this is what has killed the other men." He had a neck bone of the mountain sheep with skin sewed over it. He had it in his pocket. He had an erection and put it in with his hand until the teeth of vaginas were worn off. He did this to the first girl. He had a spirit power inside him so it made the other girls OK. He had intercourse then and it was OK so called the others. Coyote rushed in to be the next one and the others all came and did it too with all of the other girls.

After they had done this, the sun said, "I have a pet, a female antelope; I want to race it with yours." The brothers had a doe, middle-sized. They were going to race it to Moon Rock [on the Walapai Reservation] and around the rock four times and back to the house. Sun's antelope started out first. The doe didn't start until the other had a good start. The doe started bounding along but didn't run. Sun said that his pet was a good runner, and if it went around four times and back he would beat. Older Brother said, "My pet isn't running yet. Wait until mine gets started running. She'll go around four times and from there she will come back alone. Wait till she starts running." Sun said, "Mine is about to go around the rock and yours is only halfway. Why doesn't yours come back so I can kill you?" The brother said, "Mine hasn't started yet. Mine will jump over two or three washes at a time and will beat yours yet." Sun shouted out, "My antelope is three times around the rock and yours is only going around the first time." The brother said, "My doe hasn't started yet; wait 'til her fourth time around and she will start running and will jump two or three washes and will beat yours." Sun said, "My antelope is four times around and yours is only three times. Mine will be back by the time yours will go the fourth time. Then I'll kill you." Sun shouted out, "Mine is nearly halfway home and yours has just gone around four times." Older Brother said,

"Mine is going to start running now. Yours will stay about halfway and mine will come like the wind." Then the deer really started coming. Antelope was winded and tired and wasn't making much progress. The Brother said, "Yours is tired and mine is really running and will beat yours." Sun said, "You really mean it. Your doe is nearly past mine. I see it with my own eyes. That's the end of it." The deer got back to the house first but the antelope wasn't nearly home yet.

The sun said, "You beat me on that, but I can think of something else. We'll try the same course and race." He called his fastest runners. After he set the plan they agreed. So the sun's runners started out and built a fire a short distance away and the brothers started out slow. They passed the place where [they saw the] ashes of the fire of the other runners. The sun called out, "They'll lose the race. Why didn't they give up and let me kill them to use their blood to stripe myself." Before the brothers started they whispered to Coyote and told him they would go easy until they went around the rock four times, and said when they were starting home Coyote should pull the sun down from his roof, kill him and cut his heart out, and when he saw them coming, start running with them. Sun's runners went around the rock four times. When the brothers had gone around two or three times they met the others and talked. Older Brother said, "We'll let them run hard at first and we'll take it easy so they'll be tired out before we are." When they met the other team it was tired and they were looking for shade, tongues hanging out. A coyote was with them. They said, "We aren't going to stop at Sun's house but just pass by." They said to Coyote, "You look tired out," and teased him. The coyote got mad and threw a rock and hit Older Brother on the back of the head. Blood came out and is a darker color on "squaw's" head from that today. But they kept on running and passed all the fast runners. When they got near, Coyote pulled the sun down and killed it, but instead of cutting through the belly and getting the heart, he cut the shoulder and got the arm instead. Older Brother got after Coyote and said, "You did the wrong thing. You won't even survive." After he said that the sun's house was in flames. The sun was still alive. Coyote had taken the right arm and left the left arm. Sun leaned against the post of the house. He took a stone knife and rubbed against his cheek and set his house on fire. The fire spread out after the people. It nearly caught up with them so they were afraid. They asked the pines, pinyons, and other green trees if one would do them a favor and not burn so they would be saved. The trees said, "Even if we are green we still burn." They asked a rock if it would not burn so they could get inside and be saved. The rock said if it was in the fire it would get hot and split into chips. They reached some water and asked if it could protect the people. It said, "If I get in the fire I'll get hot and cook the meat." After they passed the water they asked a small bush for shelter and it said, "I won't burn, except maybe the top part." They didn't believe him. They went on and asked an ant where his house was, and if he would burn easy. The ant said it wouldn't burn because he lived down in the ground far below. The people said, "That is what we want to hear." The people went inside but the last one in was a rabbit. As the fire swept by it singed his back and made a brown spot along his back. The people were saved from the fire in the ant's house.

The people stayed there for a long time. Older Brother said, "I don't know how it is on top. I want the fly to see how it is, if the ashes are cooled." The fly went out and found it was cold. He reported back, but Older Brother didn't believe it. He sent the bee out, and he found the same thing. He went back and told them nothing was left. They said, "OK, we'll go out. Before we go out I want everyone to stay together until I say so. No one should say I came from that way or that way until I say it is OK."

There were many different animals. They came out one at a time and all waited for the others until all had left the ant's house. Older Brother said, "Now it is time to separate. Everyone can go the direction they came from. My brother and I will stay around here and not return where we came from and will turn into the squirrels." After everyone had departed for their homes, they stayed and turned into the squirrels and are still around yet.

The Man Who Caught Himself in the Eagle's Nest

A group of people lived in a village. It was in early fall when game was fat. They waited on the chief to tell them when to hunt. He would rise early, tell the men to get ready so they could cover big country.

One morning the chief arose and said to the men, "All you menfolks, we start out hunting today. Anything you find bring in and we'll roast together. On big animals we'll roast and cut them in pieces. We'll have to leave." He pointed out a direction [in which a] man had an eagle nest in a high cliff. The man said, "Take me out to that high rim. From the top, I have a rope to hang myself down to that eagle nest to get feathers for my arrows. This time of year the young should leave the nest but are still there." The men hollered agreement. By sunrise they had the man to the top of the high cliff. The men were glad he spoke; they wished for him to speak like that because when he (the chief) hunted with them he ran ahead and shot rabbits and claimed himself a good sharpshooter. The men planned to lower him to the nest and drop the rope to him and leave him there. They did it. When he was in the nest, they dropped the rope and hollered, "Watch out, we missed the rope." The man didn't answer. He knew he was going to stay there.

The men left him (the chief), and hunted over big country. The chief had two wives who asked when they returned from hunting what happened to their husband. The men didn't answer but left the wives at their home. They went around among themselves and said, "When he gets out of there he will kill us all; let's move out of here."

The next morning they all packed up and moved south. They left the two wives in the village alone. One was pregnant, and they decided not to stay. No one had told the wives what happened to their husband, but Coyote was in the group and told them their husband was in an eagle's nest and was killed there. So they were all leaving, as it was a dead man's place. All went south from there. Then the wives packed up and started following the villagers. In the evening some gathered brush for open-sided shelters for camp. Late in the evening the two wives reached the camps and stopped a little distance away. The men had hunted rabbits, brought them in, dug pits, built fire, and put rocks in it to roast [the meat]. The two wives stayed away but early next morning some leaders got up and asked some of the people to uncover the roasted rabbit, divide it, and take it to the camps to eat. The two wives were far off but heard it, and started to walk to the group where they were dividing the meat. The others pushed them back because they were selfish. When the chief was with them, they had been selfish with others, so the group wanted to treat them the same. The group tore their clothes off, and the two wives sat down and didn't try to get any meat.

After eating, the group moved off. The women got up, fixed their dresses, gathered bones from the camps, pounded them fine and ate bone meal. They followed the others.

The same thing happened. The group kept moving into country full of animals, but it was dry. They found no good water or wood, so they kept moving on all winter, spring, and summer. The woman had her baby during that winter.

The next winter during an early snowfall two families (Gila Monster and Bat cousins lived together) lived not too far from the high cliff where the chief was stranded. The chief was in the eagle nest an entire year. In fall, Gila Monster and Bat saw snow on the ground that would show tracks. One hollered, "We have first snow on the ground. Let's get up and track rabbits." They had breakfast and started out for the high cliff.

The chief saw them hunting below the cliff. He wished for good food. He was starving although he had been eating what the eagle brought for its young. He had diarrhea from that food and his flesh had shrunk away to bones. He made a song: "My grand-father, Gila Monster, will you take me down and take me home?" They heard it but were too far to tell what it was. So the chief sang, "My grandfather, Bat, I'm in a bad place. I want help. If you live near here take me home with you." Gila Monster and Bat heard the noise. They asked each other what it was, and decided to investigate. They walked close to the cliff and prayed in talking to the cliff to make a pathway to the eagle's nest. Gila Monster and Bat sat and smoked. Gila Monster said, "I'm a good one for that. I'll make a high wall crack to the eagle's nest." He smoked and blew against the high, hard wall like Hopis do, four times. All at once the hard wall had a crack from the ground to the nest. Gila Monster said to Bat, "See that. I told you I could do that." When Gila Monster saw this place he wanted first chance to climb up; he wanted to get eagle feathers. Gila Monster said he would try it first; Bat said, "O.K." Gila Monster started climbing in the crack. He had his best suit of clothes. When Gila Monster got five or six feet below the nest, he made a move once in awhile but the crack had narrowed too much to let him pass through. He wanted to go farther. He rested awhile and tried again but was squeezed tight. Finally he had to come down. At the bottom when he came down, he had some silver buttons along his leggings wrapped on his legs. He looked at it and saw holes rubbed in it and said, "I almost lost my conchos." Marks are now on the Gila Monster from that. Gila Monster sat down and rested. He said, "My cousin, I don't want to tear my dress-up clothes. You'd better try."

Bat was supposed to be a good climber. "I'll try, but I won't say I'll make it. If I don't make it we'll have to go home." Bat started. He had wings which he could flop against the sides. He came to the hard place and had just room enough to get through so he got to the nest. Bat had a burden basket. He reached into the nest and gathered the bony body into his basket. The man sang to Bat, "I collect the full [eagle] wings, sew them together and make for someone to use. If you care for it, take it to pay and pack me down." Bat looked away; he wanted another kind. The man had woven the tail feathers together in a blanket. He sang to Bat to take this for pay for the trip down. Bat said nothing.

Later the man sang and offered snowy white, downy feathers. He wanted to keep them but finally offered them to Bat. Bat said, "OK, I'll take them. Put them at the bottom of my basket with the other feathers on top." The bony body had all but his head covered by feathers. Bat started to lift the basket, but told the man, "Don't have your eyes open while we are descending or we will fall off. I'll tell you when we reach the bottom, then open your eyes and we'll both be safe." The chief said, "OK."

Bat took the loaded basket and started down. The chief kept his eyes shut almost all the way. Then he thought, "Bat is taking me to another place. If he took me the way he came up we should be there." He kept thinking this and finally had to open his eyes. Both fell off the cliff. The basket fell over Bat, and he was badly crippled; his legs and wings were all broken. Bat asked the chief to fix his bones for him and he would take care of him; but if he didn't help Bat they couldn't go anywhere. Bat was groaning with pain. A few minutes later the chief said, "All right, I'll try to fix you up." He rubbed his hands all over Bat's face, rolled dirt from outside of his own skin and made it into mud and plastered it against the broken places of Bat's bones. It healed up right away. Bat said, "I'm all right now. I'll try to pack you where Gila Monster is, just a little distance from here." He did it, and from there

Gila Monster helped him pack the chief to their camp. They fed him. He was alive but poor and skinny. They kept him there awhile until he was strong again like day.

One morning he told Bat and Gila Monster, "I'd better leave you. I want to take a trip. I want to get home. If they aren't going away, they may be at home. I want to find out. If they are gone I won't know what to do. I'm better. I want to go."

Bat and Gila Monster said, "OK."

He went home and found the deserted campsites. It looked like the people had left right after they left him in the nest. He searched for clues to the direction they had gone. He decided, and followed until he came to an old campsite. He stayed there, even though he came to it early in the evening. He went around to all the camps. He started a fire where chiefs were. In those days they had a long stone at one end used for a pillow. Anytime during night if a man went sound asleep, his head would roll off and keep him alert in sleep. The chief found all the pillow stones and got an idea from this. He tried to get their thinking from the rocks so he could kill them without help. The next day he went on to the next camp. Day after day, he did this till he came to a camp where some of the brush was still green. Then he overtook them. He found his wives.

When he came to the fresher campsites, he found out that his wives made their camp separate. He saw the baby's footprints; saw it was almost a year old and could walk from one wife to the other. He was glad and wished it were a boy. He sang these thoughts to himself.

When he caught up with his wives, the baby looked back and hollered to its father. One wife said, "What did the baby say? It sounds like he saw someone and called 'Father.'" They looked back and saw him. They dropped their packs and sat down to wait. He caught up and said, "Where are you going? I cover big country and just caught up; I didn't see anyone. Why did they leave our home?"

One wife said, "They wanted to get away from you. They were scared you will come and kill them all. They wanted to find a new home."

The chief said, "OK, I know about what they are thinking. Let's go ahead and make your camp as usual, but I won't join you until early in the night." He rested there until late in the evening, then arose and walked on to his wives' camp. He saw that his wives' dresses were ragged. So he took some of the sinew the women had, twisted it into a string and made a belt to put around their waists. He made it strong.

The next morning the men called for the people to get meat from the roasting pits and divide it. "We'll keep moving on our way." The people got meat and piled it up. The two wives came with a fruit basket, stooped to gather meat, and put it in their baskets. The men tried to tear their dresses as before, but it was hard and tight on them. The men suspected the chief had caught up. They walked off with baskets of meat. The men decided to go to their camp and see if the chief was there. They came and saw the man bouncing his baby and playing with it. He didn't see them and they sneaked away and spread the word among the people.

He planned to make a shiny ring around the outside of camp with everyone inside it and kill them all. He said to his wives, "Stay here. I'm going to visit them and pretend friendliness, but I want to kill all my leaders because they treat me bad. I'm really mad but will act friendly like always."

He walked to their camp, straight into the middle. As he came up he heard the leaders saying that the chief looked friendly, "But we know he is on war. Let's get ready to fight him." The speaker began hollering and yelling. All the people acted like lightning had hit them. People were flying up in the air and hit the ground, but the chief stood where he was. When all had hit the ground, he ran to them, hit them in the head, killed all the women and kids too. He collected the heads of all the leaders and brought them home and hung them up in a tree near his own camp.

He told his wives to dry those fat men and women, to skin and dress them, and boil the meat. "After it is cooked I want to eat the bodies. By doing that I do that as a chief."

His wives were scared but did not refuse. They started to obey him. When about half were in the pot, the man started eating them one by one from the pot. The wives kept putting meat in the pot, working around to get partly done meat. He filled up, pushed his stomach down, ate more till up to his neck, and put his finger in and pushed it down. When he was all filled up he told his wives, "Quit boiling it. I'm filled up. I'm almost ready to go to the toilet but I can't get up. There is a cliff nearby. One of you get my head, one my feet, with the baby underneath, and pack me to the edge of the high wall. It would be smelly in this camp so I want it to go down over the cliff." So they did as he said. They got to the high cliff; the walls were very high. The man told them to move real close to the edge and put him down. "I don't want just my hind on the ground but over the edge so it will go over the edge." They packed him so close to the edge they nearly fell off. He said, "OK, let me down." Then just before they put him down he kicked a little and reached with his hands for the other wife so all lost their balance and fell off the high wall.

During the night they turned into stars, and near morning, they started climbing the wall. They made a constellation of a good hunter.

(During the story the man is occasionally referred to by name. The leaders of the group have names like Bluejay, Good Hunter Hawk, Small-bird-that-has-a-head-like-a-bluejay, and Bird-that-has-a-head-like-Bluejay-with-a-sharp-crest-at-the-top. The consultant said this was a headdress and showed that he was a leader when he was human. He turned into a star and still the star kills any birds. The chief is the only one who sings. He sang in the nest to Gila Monster and Bat, and also when traveling behind the villagers, but there was no song at first when he told the hunters to prepare for the hunt. He was the principal chief and had some lesser chiefs in the village. He was not identified with any animal or human, although others in the group were birds. Coyote was the only animal mentioned, but the informant thought Bear, Wolf, and Lion took part also.

The teller can lengthen the story by repeating the day-by-day journey of the villagers. The same thing happened each day for a year. The teller doesn't repeat for four days. It is up to his whim, depending upon whether he wants to make it long or short. He usually tells it two or three times with full repetition, then says it happened like this for one year. On the husband's journey to overtake the villagers, the first day is told in detail, as is done again on the day he caught up. If the teller gets tired he can omit some details all through any story.)

Bear's Wife

Bear and his wife had a number of children, half grown, mostly girls. They lived at one camp. Each day Bear went out hunting; he never failed to go out. He started in the mornings and returned in the evening with a bunch of bones wrapped in shoots from Mormon tea plant. He brought them for his wife and kids to eat. The only other food they had was grass food gathered by the wife and the big girls.

Bear kept bringing this. His wife would pound it up on a grinding rock. Before it got too fine, bones would fly up and scatter around the ground rock. The larger girls would sit around and fight over the bones that flew up. They wished for meat, and ate every scrap, even if it fell on the ground.

Bear went to the country where there were many badger holes. He worked all day to dig out a badger, one or two of the biggest game he found. He built a fire, roasted it, ate the meat, and every day brought home only the bones.

The wife and kids were starving for meat. Finally one day the wife thought to herself whether it would be wise for her to go to her nearest neighbor, Lion, who was a good hunter. It was quite far. She wanted to marry him, not visit. She was starving. So after a few days she went to Lion's house. He had piles of fresh meat, fat, dried meat; much of it. She went in and wanted to see if he wanted to marry her. He saw her and said he wished to have a wife as he had much meat to cook and prepare for storage. He had to hunt and it kept him too busy trying to hunt and cook too. The lady was feeling just right the way the lion treated her.

Next day the bear hollered outside to see if his wife was there. He wanted her to come down and come home. The lady was in a high building, four stories, and was on the top floor cooking meat. She told him the doors were closed.

Bear waited awhile. Mountain Lion came home. Bear asked Lion to let the lady go as it was his wife. Lion said, "You can't take her back. She is my wife now." Bear asked Lion to come down and put on a fight. If Bear was killed he would come alive four times; his heart was made that way. Lion thought Bear must be powerful and said, "I don't want to fight with you." Lion said, "I can't let you take her now. I call her my wife." Lion said, "I'm a powerful man like you. I can come alive eight times." Bear called Lion to come down. Lion said, "OK, but wait till I change my clothes." This was so the bear couldn't tear up his clothes. Lion put on a suit of blue granite [limestone], then a suit of red sandstone, one of red jasper, and one of white limestone, one on top of another. This is why the canyon is this way from the bottom to top layers.

Lion came out and Bear was ready for a fight. Bear started to reach around Lion's waist. Lion did the same and bit Bear's neck, chewed it nearly in half. Then he pushed Bear away, killed him, cut him in four pieces, and threw four quarters in four directions. Lion thought that by scattering the quarters Bear couldn't come alive.

But next morning Bear was standing at the bottom of the building. He called his wife to come down and go home. His wife answered in song, "I'm not going home with you. I have found a good home, lots of meat, and good clothes. If you want to marry again, go back and marry one of your daughters. I am not willing to go back."

Then she made another song: "I have a good time here. I don't like to make love with you. Your penis hurts me. It is small and crooked at the end like a cane and hurts my vagina. I'm not coming back."

Then Lion came down for another fight. He had taken his suits of rock off, so he put them all on again and went out. Bear grabbed him around the waist but Lion chewed Bear's neck again. Lion said, "I did this way yesterday. How come you are alive?" He cut him up and threw him away as before.

This was repeated all again on the third day. The lady sang the same song. Lion killed Bear as before. Lion began to think every time the wind blew during the day that the wind pushed the quarters together and healed them up.

Lion looked for red jasper after killing Bear. He found a good one. He told his wife, "We'll try it this way." So, next morning Lion heated the jasper and told his wife to keep the fire good so the rock would be red hot. So when Bear came around [all the details of the fight were repeated].

Bear grabbed Lion around his waist. Bear tried to wrestle like a person. Lion bit him under his chin and chewed his windpipe. After killing the bear, he split the body in four pieces, but the fourth time he cut the heart out and threw the four pieces away. He took the heart and sliced it in flat pieces. The jasper was red hot and Lion put the rock over the heart pieces which were like slices of meat. He rolled the rock up in the heart and put it away in a room where it would be cooked. Lion thought Bear without a heart could never come alive again.

Next morning Lion waited for an hour for Bear to return but all was silence. That was the end of Bear.

(Lion and his wife sang in this story, but Bear did not. Lion sings the first day Bear comes to their house, telling Bear that he isn't looking for a fight but if Bear wants to fight, he is willing. He sang it on each of four days. The story is told with Bear's wife's song first sometimes; on other occasions, Lion's song is first, depending upon the storyteller.)

Turkey (or Eagle)

(This story may be told with one or the other as the central character.)

This was in a time when animals and birds were human. Turkey and his wife had a home somewhere near Cataract Canyon. His wife had relatives like a small bird around rocks (rock wren). The wren lived nearby as a neighbor. Another bird who lived in a cactus and made a hole for his nest, lived also as a neighbor. Another neighbor was a small bird that makes a noise like grinding, like a woodpecker but smaller than a flicker. There were also a few other birds who lived in the neighborhood.

One year in the fall when the days began to grow cold and early snowstorms came, the wife asked Turkey to block up the holes in the house for her to stay in. The nights were cold and windy and she couldn't do good work when she tried to grind food. The wind blew the fine seeds away. She asked him to face the door east as the wind came almost always from the other three directions. Turkey fixed the house they were in. Turkey thought it might be true. In the fall it looked cloudy like it might rain so he filled the holes up. He brought more logs to repair their home. Turkey didn't think his wife was just trying to make it appear he was lazy. He fixed the house, and after it was done his wife roasted food. She roasted grass seeds in a tray with coals by tossing it in a basket. When [the seeds were] roasted she said, "My grinding stone isn't good to do this; it is too fine. I'll take this to my uncle's place. His stone is rough enough." She went to do it. Turkey suspected nothing. Later she did this again; each time she went to a different neighbor's house.

Turkey thought it over about the grinding rock, so he pounded it all over with jasper to make it rough. But each time she continued to go to her neighbors and said she didn't like her own stone. One day she did this same thing again and said, "I'll go to Rock Wren's house. I can do it faster there." It always took her quite awhile to come home. Turkey thought he would sneak up on his neighbor's house and see what his wife was doing all that time. So he followed a few minutes after she left and peeked into a little hole in the wall. His wife was doing nothing, but Rock Wren had some rope or strings on each leg of his wife and had her legs spread out tied to the house posts. Rock Wren was starting to get on her. Turkey watched them awhile but said nothing. When his wife returned he said nothing to her. Later Turkey was feeling bad and wished to do away with his wife. He planned ahead to do it without making trouble in the neighborhood.

One morning he got up and said to his wife, "I want to see if my arrows are straight enough to shoot with." He held it up and sighted down it carefully, looking toward the door. Later he tried it in the bow, pointing toward the door. Later in the morning when the sun was high he got up, said nothing, but pulled the bowstring as hard as he could and shot an arrow out through the door. He took his lion-skin blanket for a bed and said nothing. But his wife knew he was leaving her. He followed his arrow, found it and picked it up. His wife followed him. He walked all day, and in the evening he killed a few cottontails. He found a place to stop where there was dry wood for a camp fire. He dug a hole, gathered small rocks and sticks in the hole, and skinned the cottontails. He was tight with his food. He wouldn't throw anything away in case his wife would come along and get it. He threw the skins and insides in the fire and waited until the flames died down to coals. Then he put the cottontails on some rocks, covered them with dirt, and waited for them to roast.

Early at night after dark, his wife caught up with him and came to his camp. She asked him, "Why are you leaving our house? Before you said anything you just took off and came this way. What are you mad about?" He turned his face away, half feeling bad, and acted like he heard nothing. She sat down close to him. He ignored her, and acted like he was alone. He wrapped up in his blanket. She came over and asked to get in the blanket with him. He said, "Don't bother me. I want to sleep."

Toward morning Turkey made a song. "I am going on a
long trip. You stay where we used to live. I am going where my
relatives are in a land where there is snow and ice on the mountains. Go back where we used to live if you want to but don't
bother me. I am going to a place where it is dangerous."

The next morning he gathered sticks for a fire and took the
rabbits out of the coals. He wasn't hungry for all [of them] but
took a few bites from each one and threw the rest in the fire. He
piled more wood on until all the meat and bones were burned up.
He was mad over what he had seen. Then he started on his way.

Now his wife was mad too. She hadn't got to his bed in the
night. She decided to follow him again. He did the same as
before, killed cottontails in the evening, gathered small sticks and
a big log to keep the fire all night. He made a hole for roasting
(and repeated his actions as before). He kept this up across the
country until he reached the San Francisco Peaks where most of
the turkeys live.

Then he sang, "Lady, you'll have to return to our former
home. People are waiting for you. You have many relatives back
there. I don't want you to die on my trail. I don't want you anymore. I am going to my relatives, and I live in a dangerous place.
If you die on my way, some of your relatives would say I killed
you, and they would kill me and throw hot ashes in my mouth. I
don't want to die by hot ashes. Go back."

Every morning he made this song. But she kept following.
Still he didn't want to give her any food. He kept on thinking of
what she had done and kept on his way.

Soon he was near the San Francisco Peaks, an icy-looking
mountain. He sang again that morning, "I'm near my relatives. I
don't want you to die here. Go back." And he repeated the rest of
the song.

(Turkey sang a song occasionally in evening, also. If the
storyteller wants to quiet noisy children he can repeat this song
until they are asleep. Then he can continue with the story. It can
be repeated according to the whim of the teller and occasion. The
journey is not described in detail; no place-names are given. Consultant has never counted how many days the journey took.)

The last day Turkey made a song in the morning again. This
time Turkey said, "I might run across one of my relatives before
evening comes so you'd better go back. It is dangerous for you

here. The clouds are on the mountain. I can't see the top part of the mountain, and it may rain today. I don't want you in a dangerous place."

That evening before sundown Turkey found a little draw on the foothills of the mountain. He saw a pine tree taller than others. It had few limbs but was tall. He thought it would be a good place for a fire. He dug a hole for the fire to roast cottontails. He made the fire, but gathered only enough wood to keep the fire a little while. Late in the night he wanted to sleep. He looked for his wife to show up. He thought if she showed up this would be the night she would freeze.

The wind blew hard; it blew gravel and sand into his face. He sat close to the fire for awhile. It started to snow. Heavy clouds were in the sky, and snow was moving toward where he was. By the time snow reached his camp his wife came in late like she always did. He let the fire die out as always. Wind and snow was blowing hard through the little canyons. Turkey was ready to go to bed before the fire died down. He turned himself into a real turkey and flew up to the dead limb under the branches of the tender tip of the tree protected by bushy branches.

His wife went around the tree trunk trying to get away from the wind. She asked him to take her up there with him. She kept talking to him because she knew she was going to freeze.

By the middle of the night she quit talking, and he knew she was dead. He stayed up there and waited till early morning. He saw the snow was as high as bushes. He saw his wife was frozen dead. She was pregnant. He began to think for his plan; it was better.

He gathered wood for a fire, scraped snow away from her body, moved her close to the fire, turned it around once in awhile to keep from burning her and thawed her out. By that time, her stomach got that heat and bloated up like a balloon and broke open. From there many young animals ran out from her stomach. He thought she had been with many different men. He tried to hit them all: birds, coyotes, bear, and others. He tried to kill some, but the rest ran under the snow. There was only one young turkey in the whole bunch. He said to himself, "This is my baby. I want to take him along." He killed some others, but some escaped.

He took the young turkey and started climbing the mountain. He said to himself, "My parents used to say that halfway up the east side of this mountain is a high cliff where my relatives lived. I want to see if that is the right place." He came to the top and looked down the other side and saw smoke rising from the other side from fires of his relatives.

Later he packed the young turkey down to the place where his relatives were gathered. He mixed with his relatives there.

Turkey (version 2)

[This is a shorter version of the previous story.]

Turkey built a big house where he lived with his wife. Turkey's wife said her grinding stone was no good. "I can't grind corn here. I'll have to go over to that neighbor's place. (The neighbor was a small bird with a white throat.) He has a stone that is rough and will grind good." She went to that place. Turkey followed her, saying to himself, "I wonder what she does over there every day?" Turkey's wife went inside where *Thu-tit* was. Turkey peeked in through a hole and saw his wife and *Thu-tit* making love. Turkey returned home. Two or three days passed by, and Turkey walked off toward the south for a long way. He looked around and saw that his wife was following. Turkey's wife caught up with him, and Turkey began to sing. His song said, "I have to go to bad places. It is cold there. What are you doing, you follow me all the time? You've got to go back and see your friend. You told me *Thu-tit* has a good place, nice and warm. You've got to go back." He walked on toward the south but his wife still followed. A storm came up, windy cold. Turkey flew up to the middle of a pine tree. His wife stayed down below.

Turkey built a fire in the tree and made himself comfortable. His wife called out, "Come and get me." She kept calling this. After awhile she was quiet, so he thought she was asleep and came down to get her. He tried to wake her, but she was already dead, frozen. Turkey gathered wood and built a fire. He placed her body close to the fire. After awhile the heat expanded her belly and it burst open. Many birds and animals came out: lion, rattlesnake, lizard, snake, and others. But there was just one turkey. Turkey got this little turkey and the other animals went off somewhere. They lived there for awhile, and the young turkey grew up and flew away.

Fox and the Giant Bird

[This story is sung first, then spoken.]

In the beginning, when animals were human, there were two boy foxes. They lived in a camp without a mother, because their mother had been killed or carried off along with other people by enemy raiders. But the boys had been overlooked.

The boys wondered where their mother had gone. Along in the evening the boys were hungry. The smaller one was still in the cradle. The older one was looking in all directions wishing for his mother to show up. The older one didn't know what to feed the younger boy. Then he saw some young birds run around near the door of the house, but he didn't understand just how to kill them. They had eaten nearly all the food in the house. The boy threw small rocks at the birds and crippled them but didn't kill them. Then he took a small stick, held a rock against the end of it, and flipped it. He would kill a bird once in awhile that way. He knew that his mother used to dig a hole under ashes to cook, so he did it that way to get the meat done. Then he picked off what meat the little birds had in them and put it in a bighorn mountain sheep dipper with a little water and salt and fed this to his younger brother to suck the juice. He knew that his little brother would stay alive and grow up that way. He repeated this every day for awhile.

The boy thought his mother had gotten lost; she used to gather grass food and firewood and then come back; he wondered where she could be.

The boys grew, and later on tried to make a bow and arrow. Once in awhile they killed birds around camp. The older brother thought of making a trap for mice, rats, and jackrabbits. There were many around. Older Brother thought awhile about it and formed sinew to make string with inside the house. He spun it into string and began to make traps. First he trapped a mouse, then rats. The next morning he got a cottontail and the next morning a jackrabbit. Every morning he told his younger brother to look in the trap and see what was making the noise. Every morning it got bigger and bigger: mountain lion, bighorn mountain sheep, deer, elk, buffalo. Way at the end he saw a big animal with wings like an eagle, but bigger yet. Younger Brother tried to hit the eagle with rocks to kill it, but it was hard to kill it. It was about as big as an airplane. He couldn't find a way to kill it, so he returned and asked his older brother to come and find a way to kill it. Both threw rocks and shot it with a bow and arrow. But each time the point of the arrow bumped off the animal's hide. Older Brother said, "We have no way to kill him. It looks like he is going to come toward us and get us." They kept trying to kill it until the sun was in the middle of the sky. The bird came toward them and scooped them up on its wings and carried them off to an island in the ocean where he had many other people.

The bird alighted and let them off his wings. Younger Brother was glad to see all the people. He joined in games and had a good time. Older Brother thought maybe this bird had got his mother, and he didn't like to live on an island surrounded by water. The other people didn't think that way; they just had a good time.

Older Brother thought about what to do until he had an idea. Then he went to the place where the people were playing games and called for them to stop and listen. He said, "This is no good. He dumped us all in here with no way to escape. I think he is going to eat us all. You don't think of that. I have a plan to escape." He called the duck to go under water and gather small, sharp obsidian stones. Then he spread out a tanned buckskin. The duck said, "Yes, I can do that." He jumped in the ocean and gathered obsidian and brought it to the people.

One of the birds went on dryland, got an elk horn with a sharp end, and used it to flake obsidian into small sharp pieces. When he was finished they chose a small child who had no mother or father, so Older Brother pointed him out to be killed. Then they smashed his body so it would be bloody. They put rocks inside his body and roasted him. Then they fed it to the cannibal bird. They gave the boy's body to an old blind lady who fed the cannibal bird. Then they carried out the plan. The bird returned without any more victims. It said, "I'm pretty tired. I want to eat and drink water." The old lady said, "I have nothing for you except this body here that others have cooked up for you." He said, "This looks good." He started eating, chewed a little but felt nothing. After awhile he cleared his throat so the lady knew he was about to die.

Before they gave the body to the animal, the fox asked the people, "Which one of you can dig a hole big enough for all of us to hide in? Before the bird dies he will rub his wings together and will mash us all. The badger said he could do it. The prairie dog dug a hole for the old lady so she could drop into it. Badger dug for the other people.

Before the bird died, it rubbed its wings together, but could find no one as the people were underground. Then, before he quit rubbing, the bird dropped over and made a big noise like falling timber.

The fox said, "I think maybe he is just pretending. Let's wait awhile." Then he sent the ant out to see.

The ant went and crawled around and stung the bird's legs but the bird didn't move. He returned and said it was dead. The fox said, "I don't think he is really dead." He sent the bee out to see. The bee flew around, stung the bird on its legs and over its body, but the bird didn't move. He returned and said it was really dead.

The fox said, "OK, I'll take the lead. You follow me, as he might kill me." They came out. The people saw the fox was using his head and killed the animal like it was a small one.

The fox said, "Now he's dead, but we must find a way to get off this island. We can take the longest feather and throw it across to see if it will reach the land. From there we can return to our homes."

One of the men used a sharp rock to chop off the feathers. He raised one end and shoved it off, but it didn't quite reach land. He tried another feather a little longer and it reached dryland.

The fox said, "I'll take the lead. I want you all to wait on the mainland while I talk to you." The people said, "All right. You used better judgment than the rest of us. We'll do what you want."

When they all reached the other side they gathered around the fox, and he said, "We must not leave here today. We must wait till dawn tomorrow. I'll make a speech, then you must all go in different directions to your homes."

The next morning the fox made a speech. He said, "We made a good plan to kill the bird. I know you all want to return to your homes. You know the way from where the bird brought you. My brother and I will claim this stretch along the ocean where grapevines and other kinds of food grow. Any animal like us that stays by the ocean or rivers must be called Fox."

The people all left for their own homes. The two brothers stayed there and turned into foxes.

Fox and His Brother

[This is another version of the preceding tale.]

The fox and his brother were living with some other people in a
village to the west. When they hunted they couldn't get enough to
eat so the fox and his brother decided to go away from there to
another place. When they left they camped at night; then the next
day they started setting out traps. They didn't have traps but
made them with a flat stone on top set at an angle and held up by
a stick. They used bait from a prickly pear before the blossom
comes on and sinew to tie it. After they had trapped there, they
went on toward Ashfork [about seventy miles south of Supai village on the southern edge of aboriginal Havasupai territory] and
stayed there; they liked the place. They said to each other, "This
looks like a good trapping place." They liked it because they
could trap mice, rats, squirrels, and small animals. The next day
after they had gotten many small ones, they got a cottontail rabbit and liked it because there was enough for the next day. They
set traps in the evenings, and the next time caught a jackrabbit.
The next night (the third) they got a bobcat. The next time was a
mountain goat (sheep). This time there was enough that they
could dry it. The next it was an antelope. Next was a deer. Next
was an elk (same kind of trap).

After they got all the big things, they caught a hawk but
they didn't eat it, they just used the feathers for arrows. Next they
caught *čuⁿda*, a hawk that swoops swiftly and makes a popping
sound [night hawk]. The next was an eagle, *kaⁿčuⁿda*, but he did-
n't die so they killed him. They used the same trap for birds as for
animals. The next night they set the trap, but this time after they
went to bed they heard something like thunder. Older Brother
heard it first and listened for a long time. He woke Younger
Brother and said, "Sounds like something very large in the trap.
Sounds like it might get us." Younger Brother went and shot at it
with arrows, but he broke all of them. He returned and got his
tomahawk, but every time he hit it, the bird raised its head again.
Its eyes were very large. Younger Brother returned and told the
older brother that he had broken his arrows and broken his tom-
ahawks and was afraid it would get them. They went back to
watch it and said, "It looks like it is going to get out of the trap."

It flew out, picked them up and put them on his shoulders and flew away to the west with them to the ocean where there was an island. He put them there where he had put many people he had carried away. Many, many people were there, playing games. The bird left them there, but they didn't join in the games. (The informant called the giant bird *miä giv²*, meaning "something big that covers the sky.") For four days the two brothers stayed by themselves and thought. On the fourth day the brothers went to the other people and talked. The older brother spoke: "You act like nothing is wrong. You play games while the giant cannibal bird is eating you up one by one. The rest of you do not think of this but think only of your games." After he said this, he said, "I want us to get together and plan what we can do." They did this. The fox told the ducks and geese to go under the water and get a chunk of obsidian so they could chip it up. He told the hummingbird to go on top of the sky and get an elk horn. They both returned with the horn and obsidian. People sat around chipping obsidian into tiny sharp flakes. They also cut the horn into small pieces and mixed it with the obsidian flakes. After they did that they said to choose one of the children who was an orphan and kill him and stuff him with obsidian flakes and horn pieces. They did this and planned to give the body to the bird's wife so she would put it on the fire to roast it and would give it to Cannibal Bird, and he would eat it and die. They took the body to the bird's wife and told her to make a tunnel so she could escape when the bird felt the obsidian inside him. The fox and the others all joined in making a tunnel to escape from the bird. After they finished the tunnel they started going into the tunnel so they would have time for all to get inside. Then they heard the bird coming. The bird came and said, "Old Lady, I'm hungry for dry meat." The lady said, "You know there is nothing, but you always say that." She just pretended like this. After awhile she went and got the body and set it before him. He cut it a little at a time and ate it in small pieces. He made funny noises, kept clearing his throat, and said, "Old Lady, it seems like I swallowed this in the wrong throat." She said, "Why don't you eat more slowly?" The bird kept eating and finally his wife saw he was about to die; his eyes were rolling back. So she fled into the tunnel. The bird had some kind of spirit to make people all over die, so he flapped his wings together in three directions but fell dead over before he could do it the fourth time. The people waited awhile and were afraid to come out. Then the fox sent a fly out to see if the bird was dead. The fly buzzed around and entered the bird's mouth, laid eggs all over its body so maggots hatched and crawled through it. The fly went back and told them the bird was dead, so they sent a bee out to see. The bee stung the bird, but the bird didn't move. The bee went back and told them the body was already spoiled and covered with maggots. So the people came out. They wondered what to do to escape from the island.

The fox was smart and said, "Let's plan something or we'll stay here forever. Let's cut the tips off the bird's wings and throw them across the water and see if it would go to the land." So they cut one wing tip and all threw together but it landed in the water a little short of the land. They tried again with the same wing and it fell short again. So the fox said, "Let's try a bigger part of the wing." They did, and threw together, and it spread out and reached the land. The fox said, "That's much better. Now let's cross it." It was like a bridge. The fox said for no one to go off in the directions they had come from until all had crossed and together could decide what to do. They started to cross and kept going and going and going. The fox was the last to cross. He saw many houses there on the land and thought to himself, "It looks like a big village." When he reached there he spoke: "We have had a bad experience with a bird that wanted to eat us. It is a wonder we all escaped. Now is the time for all of us to go to our homes in the different directions." So the people started leaving and leaving and leaving, one by one, until Fox, Younger Brother, and a few others were left. The fox said, "We'll stay in this place." When all were gone except the two brothers, they were making the noise that foxes make that sounds like *kao, kao, kao*. They said they would stay in that place and live like foxes. That kind of fox is light brown and lives near the ocean. Foxes around Supai are a darker brown.

Gila Monster and Hunter Hawk

(The entire story is sung first, then repeated in speech, sung again and spoken a fourth time. Sometimes it is referred to either as "Gila Monster" or "Hunter Hawk.")

The hawk was camped alone. A small bird came to tell him that Gila Monster had killed his relatives, Mountain Lion and Wolf, and other relatives. The relatives were sharpshooters, but they were killed. South of Walapai Mountain (south of Kingman) was Gila Monster's home. The small bird crossed the desert and came to the edge of some timber where Hawk was living on a high ridge toward Hackberry. The bird cried to the hawk. The hawk asked what was wrong. The bird didn't reply but kept crying with tears running. He finally told him, "All of your uncles were killed by Gila Monster." The hawk didn't believe anyone had nerve enough to touch lions or wolves because they were powerful, and he didn't think Gila Monster had killed them with rain. So the next day he went on as usual, hunting like nothing had happened. The bird was there when the hawk returned at evening, wanting Hawk to say something so he would take the word back. One morning Hawk asked the bird how come Gila Monster had been able to kill lions and wolves who were so much stronger than Gila Monster. But the bird was still crying as he was afraid of the hawk. The bird told him that one morning Gila Monster had rounded up his men and told them if they ran into any deer he wanted them to make a deer drive and chase them so the lions and wolves would follow the trails. Sharpshooters would wait there and kill the deer so they wouldn't have to pack the meat home. The lions and wolves were sharpshooters, so Gila Monster told them to wait along the trails for the deer, but Gila Monster wanted the main trail for himself because most deer came that way. He told the lions and wolves when they saw the deer coming they should leave it up to Gila Monster to do the shooting. A big buck came along the edge of the timber. They all saw it come up toward where Gila Monster was waiting. But somehow one of Lion's or Wolf's boys hid out in front of Gila Monster and when it came close, they had first shot at it. When it ran close by Gila Monster it fell and died. They butchered it and had a fuss over the hide. They stretched it. Gila Monster claimed the hide and said he owned the place so it belonged to him, and he put it to one side. Wolf's or Lion's boy went over and took the hide away from Gila Monster. They quarreled and got into a fight and killed the Gila Monster. This is what the small bird told the hawk. After Gila Monster died, Lion and Wolf packed the meat and hide back home. Just before they reached home a dark cloud appeared and spread over the sky; rain and hail fell. The hail was twice as big as a thumb. It knocked them down and killed or drowned them all. The small bird told the hawk this.

The hawk thought it over and thought it wise to make a plan. Toward morning Hawk told the bird to get up and run as far as he could around the world and tell what had happened and summon everyone to Hawk's camp, which everyone knew. The next day Hawk made a headdress with feathers and hide of a lower deer leg sewed together for a hat. Next he made deerskin pants, from knee down like Hopis use, wrapped buckskin, and a pair of moccasins. In four days and nights the small bird returned and said he had covered the world and everyone was coming. People had already started arriving on the first day from close by. On the morning after the fourth day, everyone had come.

The hawk made a speech and said, "We don't want to act foolish like a lady and show off by going to the place Gila Monster lives. We want to make ready and go over there and have a real man fight." All preparations were completed. The next day at sunrise Hawk was the leader and started to Gila Monster's home. They crossed into the desert and came to the middle of the desert, when one man saw a big buck antelope. They wished for some meat to eat when they camped that night. They wondered which man would be best to sneak close to the antelope. The snake and coyote were both with the group. Coyote had the snake wrapped around his neck. The snake asked Coyote to put him down so he could crawl close and poison the antelope to kill him. The Coyote said, "Don't say that. Hawk is leader and is going to get someone to go close and shoot the antelope." The hawk asked the mountain lion and wolves to try, but it was open desert and they had no way to get close. The wildcat also said, "I'm a good hunter but there is no way to sneak up." So the snake asked Hawk if he could try. The hawk said, "OK, we want meat tonight when we camp. So don't let him get away." So Coyote let Snake down. He had no feet or legs to walk. Everyone watched Snake go along the ground out of sight. After awhile the buck jumped up and ran a short distance then fell down, kicked awhile, then lay still. They thought Snake had got him, so good runners went to the antelope and saw the snake near the antelope. But the snake said, "Stay away 'til I get all of the poison out. Then you can skin and dress it." Then the snake went to the antelope and sucked all the poison out. He told them to skin and dress it. All the people gathered, prepared it by cutting it in small pieces, and packed it to the foot of the mountain near Gila Monster's home. They started fires and cooked the meat and ate it up by morning.

Before the dawn the snake made song to the coyote to wrap him around Coyote's neck and pack him to the place where Gila Monster usually made a speech to his people: a rock pile for a morning speech. He told Coyote to put him under the pile of rocks so he could kill the child of the gila monsters. Coyote said, "Stop talking like that. I don't want to pack you around for nothing." The snake kept telling him to do it, so before morning Coyote did as Snake wished. During the night Hawk asked the people to make a circle around all of Gila Monster's people. "Make a frame against our enemies sitting side by side at Gila Monster's home village. If you have more people make a second row. If more, make a third row. This will protect us so not all will be killed." He asked if anyone knew how to block Gila Monster's home (hole) in the rocks. Some men said they were good at doing that. A mouse was the one chosen to go to each camp where they had bows and arrows and chew the strings almost in two so when pulled they would break at once. The mouse did this while Hawk waited. Just before morning the mouse returned and said. "I think I cut all of them nearly in two." The men arranged themselves in three rows around the gila monsters' homes. Hawk asked a few sharpshooters to go with him and he told the rest to stay in the circles.

When the sun was almost to rise, Hawk said, "Now it's time for us to make believe we are friends traveling to the gila monster village." They started out; when they were close the sun rose and they saw some gila monsters out of bed starting fires. Some gila monster men said, "Here's some of our friends coming." The next thing they knew they saw the headdress that meant war. So the gila monsters grabbed bows and prepared to fight. The chief gila monster started for a hole, where no one could reach him. At the entrance he stopped and turned. The hawk said, "All right, let's start shooting." The gila monster shot but his arrow moved slowly and Hawk grabbed the arrow. Gila Monster told Hawk to shoot at him. Hawk wet the arrow and pulled the bow hard and shot at Gila Monster. The arrow went into Gila Monster's body at a soft place under the arm and Gila Monster grabbed at the arrow with the point sticking out the other side. Gila Monster started to run into the hole but Hawk grabbed a tomahawk and he pounded Gila Monster to death there.

The other gila monsters were still fighting, but Hawk's relatives were slow. By evening they had killed all of the gila monsters.

Meanwhile Snake was at the rock pile. When Hawk started for the gila monsters' homes, Gila Monster made a speech. Then they heard the speaker say, "Snake bite me, Snake bite me." Gila Monster killed Snake there. He had no way of coming alive. But Snake wanted it that way. He had asked Coyote for a one-way trip; he had wanted to be killed.

About midday Hawk made a speech to the people: "It is no use to run back in groups to your homes. Make a camp together and keep in one group on the desert. The next day I'll make a speech. I'm taking charge of this trip." So the people thought it right to follow him.

On the way the people gathered dead timber between Kingman and Valentine; this caused the open desert there. In the early evening they saw a cloud rising south from Walapai Mountain. It was a heavy dark cloud. It was already snowing. It hovered overhead above their camp. Snow fell heavily. By the middle of the night the fire was still going strong, but the firewood was getting low. It snowed steadily all night. The wood was all gone a little later, and only charcoal was left. They didn't know how to manage snow, so the people lay on the ashes for warmth. The people piled up on one another. The fire died out and it snowed more heavily and crowded people closer together. The snow began to cover the pile of people. Hawk looked around and saw the people already dying from the cold, so he decided to turn into a bird so he could fly and escape. So he did and flew up into the tree at the camp. It had thick limbs near the top where he could find protection. The snow got so deep it nearly covered him, too, but then it stopped snowing. Hawk stayed in the tree till morning. When the sun came up Hawk said to the sun, "A good hunter shouldn't be waiting around this time of morning." So he flew away.

Porcupine

(A story for children and adults.)

Once a porcupine lived by himself. He decided to go out hunting, to hunt a big buck to get more meat than from a fawn or doe.

The porcupine knew that during the fall of the year bucks have lots of fat on them; so he started out. He gathered arrowweeds and straightened crooked places by putting them on a charcoal fire. He used to fix a mud arrow straightener; he would heat mud in the fire, then run the arrow through and straighten it. He made many straight arrows, as many as porcupine quills and put them on his back to his shoulders and sides. He wanted to kill a buck that way. Porcupine quills turn black. He got points (obsidian) from a ridge along Rose Well. [An aboriginal pitchstone quarry has been recorded in this area.] The porcupine had arrows, but no bow. He started out from camp early and found deer signs. He traveled slowly, looking out. He went quite a ways, stopped and saw a buck lying where he thought it best for him to go. It was on the pointed end of a ridge, and he saw the horns sticking up. He decided to hide among the trees and bushes so the buck wouldn't be frightened and run away. He crept up slowly until he was near the buck. He got up close and entered the buck through its (anus). He stuck an arrow into the buck. It was hurting so he jumped up and ran. It fell dead. Then the porcupine came outside again and wanted to skin the buck. He reached around his waist for his knife and found he had left it at camp. He wondered how he could skin it. He looked around and found rocks but none were sharp. He threw one against another and made a lot of noise. He tried to break it to make a sharp edge but couldn't make a good one. He looked all around.

Then a coyote heard the noise and came to the place. He saw what Porcupine was doing and heard Porcupine talking to himself: "I forgot my knife. I don't know what to skin it with. It's a big buck. I wonder if I can find a sharp rock."

Coyote listened awhile and moved closer. He said, "Porcupine, what are you doing here? What are you missing?" Porcupine stood there kind of excited, not knowing what to say.

Then he said, "I didn't say anything. I'm looking for a sharp rock to cut a limb from this bush to make an arrow."

Coyote said, "No, I heard you talking to yourself. I know what you said."

Porcupine said, "No, I didn't say anything. I'm looking for a sharp rock to cut a limb from this bush to make an arrow."

Coyote said, "No, you didn't say that. I heard you say, 'I wish for knife, I don't know what to skin my big buck with.'"

Porcupine stood, not knowing what to say. Then he admitted it and told where the buck was, a little way back there.

Coyote felt better and began to think what he would do. Coyote said, "I'll help you skin. I have my knife." So they went to the buck. It was a big one. Coyote felt the horns and body. He saw how big it was, and he looked at it awhile. Coyote said, "Well, let's do this before we skin the buck. Let's make a line over there and run one by one and run from there and jump over the buck and see who jumps farther. The one who jumps farther we say is the one that killed the buck."

Porcupine said, "That isn't a good way. I already killed the buck." Coyote said, "Yes, let's do it that way." Finally Porcupine agreed. They drew a line. Porcupine said, "OK, you take first chance." Coyote said, "OK, watch me." Coyote ran and jumped but not very hard. He made a mark where he landed. He called back to Porcupine to get a start.

Porcupine ran and came to the buck, tried to jump, but bumped against it. He couldn't go over. Coyote laughed at him.

Porcupine said, "I'm the one that killed it. I'm not really doing it. I'll start over." So he started again but only jumped a little and bumped into it.

Coyote said, "That's enough. Let's quit."

Porcupine said, "No, I'll try again." They did, three or four times, but still he failed.

Coyote said, "This is enough." So he started to skin the buck and Porcupine sat there and watched. Coyote skinned it all. Porcupine didn't have a word to say. After Coyote finished he had to pack it away to a big tree to put it up high so the meat would be safe. After he finished, Coyote went home.

Before Coyote went home he sat at the foot of a tree and defecated there and left it to keep an eye on Porcupine so he couldn't get the meat and hide it.

Coyote called his children and his wife the next morning to go to the place where the buck was up in a tree.

When Porcupine thought Coyote was far away, Porcupine went to the tree and started to climb it to get the meat. The (feces) called to Coyote and said, "Coyote, Porcupine is reaching your pile of meat to take it away." Coyote ran back and grabbed Porcupine and threw him on the ground and killed him. Coyote said,

"Porcupine, I'm the one that killed the buck," even though Porcupine was dead.

Coyote started for home when the (feces) called him again a few times like before. Coyote returned and found Porcupine was alive again and trying to reach the meat. Coyote ran back and caught Porcupine and killed him again. He cut his shoulders and legs off and threw them in four directions. Coyote started home again. The wind blew Porcupine together again. He came alive again. He reached the meat and the (feces) called again.

Coyote returned, killed Porcupine, and threw him away again. Then the wind blew the pieces together.

On the fourth time Porcupine found a round jasper rock and thought it was a good thing to take along. He started to climb the tree again but kept an eye on the (feces) until it was ready to open its mouth to holler to Coyote. The Porcupine reached around and threw the rock into its mouth so it couldn't holler to Coyote. Porcupine got the venison and dropped it all to the ground. A little distance away he saw a pine tree. He moved all the meat halfway up the tree. He found a place to build a fire. He cooked the intestines and boiled the blood and put it in the large intestine and boiled it to drink. For awhile he did it a few days; he thought he had a good place to have a home there.

Coyote told his wife and kids he killed a big buck in the woods. "We'll have to move our camp over there." They started for the place, stopped, pointed to the tree and he told his two sons to race to that tree. He said, "The winner will get that bag of the buck hanging on a small limb."

The boys raced to the tree, looked around, but saw no meat. Coyote and his wife and the other kids came up and saw the meat all gone. Coyote thought it over and said, "I think Porcupine must have gathered it and took it away. Let's hunt it. He can't be very far." By then the boys saw Porcupine in a tree and hollered, "Here's Porcupine in this tree." They gathered at the base of the tree. Coyote hollered and asked for meat. Porcupine saw all of them below and reached for a front quarter. He told Coyote and his family to stand to one side close together. "Don't stand scattered or I might hit one of you." Coyote agreed, and all stood close together. Porcupine swung the front shoulder, made believe he would throw it to one side, but hit them all. They fell over and all fell dead. But later on Coyote's baby was crying and crawled from beneath the dead people.

"Porcupine, will you take me up there? I'm dying for meat, for soup." Porcupine had an idea to act like an old lady. He put a burden basket on his back, ran down the tree, put the baby in the basket, and climbed the tree again. Then he boiled blood in the gut; the soup was red, everything was all red. The baby was hungry. Porcupine gave soup to the baby. The baby asked for more. "I want more." Porcupine said, "OK, get all you want; fill up with the soup." Then he ate more and said, "I got enough." But Porcupine told him to eat all of the pot of soup. He said, "I've got enough." But Porcupine forced him to drink more and more till he was filled up to his neck. Then the baby asked where the toilet was. Porcupine said, "Go up to the top of the tree." He warned him it would bend but he must go to the very tip. The baby boy started up and came to the place where it bent over. He called, "Is this high enough?" Porcupine told him to go higher. The baby said, "Is this the place?" Porcupine said, "Yes, that's it." Porcupine grabbed the trunk of the tree and shook it until the baby fell and broke, scattered all over the ground. His blood turned into prickly pear with fruit all ready to gather, to fall on the ground.

Porcupine said to himself, "This is the year for prickly pear. I don't want to see it waste. I'll gather it."

He took the burden basket and went down the tree, gathered a lot of fruit, and prepared it to dry so it would keep. While doing it he said to himself, "If there is any human in this world, I'm the one that makes this cactus fruit for humans to use."

Porcupine (version 2)

[A second version of the preceding story.]

The porcupine was living in his house. He wanted some meat so he sharpened his quills and went out hunting. He saw a deer and was thinking "How will I kill it? If I get in from his (anus) I can get into his stomach and will shoot my quills out so I can make his blood run out and he will die." This was his plan. He saw the deer lying in the shade, sneaked up close, entered through the (anus) and ejected his quills so the deer's stomach filled with blood. The deer jumped up and ran, but in a short distance he dropped dead. Porcupine came out of the deer and was going to skin it when he noticed he had forgotten his knife. Porcupine walked around talking to himself saying, "I wish I had a knife so I could skin the deer." He didn't think anyone would hear him, but Coyote was hiding nearby in the bushes and heard him. Coyote came out and asked, "What did you say?" Porcupine said, "I didn't say anything. I forgot my knife. I wish I had it so I could whittle a stick." Coyote said, "No, you didn't say that. What were you saying?" Finally Porcupine gave up and told Coyote he had killed a deer and had forgotten his knife. Coyote said, "I have my knife. I'll tell you what we'll do. We'll race to the buck and the one who jumps farthest over it will be the killer and can skin it and eat it." Porcupine said, "No, I'm the killer, it's mine." But finally Porcupine gave in and agreed. They were a short distance from the buck and Coyote said, "OK, you try it first." Porcupine tried but wasn't fast enough and couldn't jump over it. Then Coyote tried, ran fast, and jumped way over it. Coyote came back and said, "I'm the one that killed the deer, so you sit there and watch." Coyote skinned it and took all the meat but the guts. He threw the guts on Porcupine's face so Porcupine ate the guts all up. Coyote tied all the meat in the deer hide and hung it up on a tree, then went home. He had a wife and children. Next morning he told them he had killed a deer and hung the meat in a tree. He told them to move camp over there to eat the meat. They did this. When they were approaching the tree, he told two of his sons he wanted them to race to the tree and the winner was to eat the kidney. When the winner reached the tree he didn't see the kidney. The sons walked around and said, "I don't see any kidney around here." Everyone came along. Coyote said, "I hung it around here." He looked up higher where the other meat had been, and it was missing too. They looked around and found a trail leading to a tall pine tree. Porcupine was building a fire up there and cooking the meat he had taken while Coyote was gone. Coyote called, "Porcupine, give us some meat." After that Porcupine said, "All right. I don't want you to scatter around, stay together in a group. He was thinking he could hit them all at once. He said, "I'm going to throw down a front quarter. If you move I might hit you." He threw it and hit them all on the neck and cut them all.

After he threw the front quarter down and killed them all, there was one baby who wiggled around under the dead bodies and finally came out from underneath and called, "Porcupine, come and get me. I want to come up where you are." Porcupine made a good path with sand to the top of the tree for the child. The child crawled up. Porcupine cooked the blood of the deer for him. The child ate and he was full. Porcupine urged him to eat more. He ate and said he was full. Porcupine urged him to eat more. Then the baby said, "Where is your toilet?" Porcupine said, "Go to the top point of the pine tree. That is where I go." So the baby started up and called, "You mean here?" Porcupine said, "No, go higher." He kept urging him until he reached a soft branch. Porcupine said, "Yes, that's where I mean." Porcupine shook the tree so hard the baby fell to the ground and burst open. The blood he had eaten ran out. From it grew prickly pear with red fruit. Later Porcupine took a basket and gathered prickly pear fruit and took it to the top of the pine tree and dried it. He lived there from that time on.

Bat

(Another Coyote story for children.)

A bat had two wives; he had a home; he had many children almost like chickens when eggs hatch. During the daytime he don't stay around the house; he gets up early in the morning, takes his bow and arrow, and goes out hunting big game: deer, antelope, mountain sheep, mountain lion. At night when he returned and came close to the house he hollered, "I'm coming, folks, with a pack of the fat on my back, so keep the flames of the fire down, just charcoals so we can roast the fat." He never returned home in the day. Regularly he came at night so he didn't show his face.

One day the bat children asked their mother, "What does our father look like? He always leaves early and returns late so we can't see his face."

So they made a plan to see what kind of person he was. The children made the plan, asked their mothers' permission, and the wives said, "OK." They hadn't seen his face either.

back and said he forgot his arrows, and called to his wife to send the middle daughter across with the arrows. The women thought something was wrong, so one said she would send the youngest daughter. But Coyote asked for the youngest. The wife sent the middle daughter. Coyote called that halfway across the water was deep and told her to pull her dress all the way up. She didn't want to, but when the water got deep, she pulled up her dress. Coyote watched and saw her naked and wanted her. When she reached his side he had sexual relations with her, his own daughter. Then Coyote went on alone and rounded up the mountain goats. When he came to the new camp, the lion and wolf asked if he had done what they told him. The girl went back to her mother and told her what Coyote had done. The mother said that Coyote was no good. The mother was thinking for awhile, "When Lion goes hunting he never stays long, so we'll have to start taking down camp before he returns." After they took down the camp, the lady said she and her daughters would turn into deer, rabbits, lizards, or any animals so there would be nothing left when Lion and Wolf returned. The mother changed her children into animals, but she decided she didn't like it because when Lion's sons hunt, they never fail to get their prey, so she decided to change them all into buffalo. The mother said that was good. Everything they owned in their house became part of their body. The roof became their fur, the fireplace stones became their hoofs, the water jug became their head, the carrying basket became their mouth, the lodge poles became their ribs, the grinding stone became their kidneys. The lady said that was good. Coyote had a small son. The mother told her daughter to put Coyote's boy between her horns so he could warn them when the hunters returned and they could turn another direction. The hunters were at their camp drying the meat, making jerky. Coyote wasn't behaving like himself. Coyote was crying and would move into the smoke every time the breeze changed it, so he could pretend the smoke was in his eyes, and they wouldn't know he was crying. Lion asked him what was wrong. Coyote said in his dreams that something was wrong at their old camp. Lion told Bobcat to go back to the old camp to see because he was sneaky and they wouldn't see him. Coyote objected that Bobcat couldn't run as fast as he could. Finally, they let Coyote go. He started off, then went another way and lay down and slept all day. Then at evening he returned and told the others that everything was OK at camp; that the women were cooking and awaiting their return. The Lion said they would return home next day. They packed their meat and started home. When they were nearing home they saw buffalo in a bunch. As they came nearer, the buffalo turned and started off southeast.

Below Desert View where the Little Colorado [River] comes in [to the Colorado River] it was level. Lion told Coyote to make a canyon there so the buffalo couldn't cross and they could kill them there and get the hide to cover a sweathouse. Coyote made the canyon, but the buffalo jumped across. Then Coyote made Redwall [limestone] of Moenkopi Wash, but the buffalo jumped across and went on their way. They went straight on southeast until they reached the big ocean. Lion told Coyote to make ice around the water so they would slip and break their legs. The buffalo kept slipping but got through, except for an old lady. The lion and others killed her after she broke her hip. Other buffalo went under the water like moose, not drowned. That is where buffalo started from, and there are still lots of them in a country somewhere. They dressed the buffalo and took out the organs and meat, then they came back toward home.

Coyote Packs a Pole

(Also called Wolf and Coyote.)

Wolf and Coyote lived together. A close neighbor was a mother bear with her young, probably four. Wolf said to Coyote one day, "We need grass food." Mrs. Bear had gathered enough at her home. Wolf sent Coyote to visit her with a gift of dried meat mixed with fat so she would repay with grass seeds. He told Coyote not to stay close to the door. Mrs. Bear went out every morning to gather food in a burden basket. When she returned, if she found Coyote at the door she might not like it as she had young to play there. So Coyote said, "OK, I'll take this blood and fat well done, boiled in guts." He thought he could make Mother Bear feel good toward them so she would give them grass food.

Wolf told Coyote not to bother her. In the evening when she returned she always put her burden basket at the door and exhaled a big breath like she was tired out. When she entered the house she always grabbed her bag of tobacco and pipe. She would start smoking the mud pipe. Wolf told Coyote, after she finished smoking she always lay on her back and used the pipe in her vagina until she had an orgasm. When she finished, she put her foot against the wall and turned all the way around several times before she finished. "I always just watch, never bother her. She may grab you if you get too close." Coyote then thought it would be a good thing to go see what would happen with him.

Wolf went hunting and Coyote started to his aunt's home, Bear Woman. About noon he came to her home. He saw the little ones playing near the door. He hung his pack on trees a little way from the house like Wolf had said, but took the blood and guts and cut them into pieces and gave some to the young bears to eat. He watched them closely until they went to sleep. Then he packed them inside and lay them side by side with a cover to sleep till their mother returned.

While they slept he took cool charcoal from the fireplace and put them in a line down the center of each child's stomach. Supais say this makes the child sleep longer.

Then Coyote went back under the tree where he could look into the house through the door, and waited.

Later in the evening Bear Woman made a sound like she was approaching the house, her claws hitting against sticks and rocks, moving slowly, so Coyote knew it was hard on her feet. She can't travel fast like other animals. She did as Wolf had said. She put her burden basket down, went inside, looked for her tobacco, lit her pipe, smoked, then used the pipe in her vagina. Coyote watched her do this but he can't wait. Pretty soon Coyote's penis was getting hard. He wanted to wait. He pressed it down, but he just can't wait. So he went to the door and whispered to her, "My aunt, this is the kind they use." So he went in and put his penis in and they had orgasm quickly. Then he tried to pull away, but she tightened her legs and tried to keep him there. Later he felt her legs loosen and tried to jump away, but she tightened up again. He said, "It's getting late. I want to go home." She did this over and over but he could never get away. Then she loosened up and he jumped up above where she lay. She reached for the soft, fleshy muscle on his back beside his backbone where the sinew comes from and grabbed this from his back. Coyote ran quickly away.

Bear got up and called, "Coyote, I've got your backbone meat."
He said, "That's not my meat. That's your red paint bag." Then
Coyote went on his way home. But Coyote really had pain in
him. By the time he reached home, he was walking crooked with
pain. When he came in and lay down, Wolf was already there.
Coyote told Wolf, "My uncle, I came to the place where you sent
me. I went there and did what you asked all the way through, but
before I left, my aunt asked me to fetch wood. She wanted a long
pole to last awhile. I looked around and found a tree with the
limbs partly broken. I broke off others and packed the tree on my
back. When nearly there I stumbled and fell and scraped the meat
off my back. So my aunt told me to come home because I
couldn't pack wood farther."

Wolf knew this was false and knew what Coyote had done
because he knew the coyote's way.

The next day he sang to Coyote, "I told you what would
happen if you fooled with your aunt. I know what you did. Next
time I send you over there, you must mind me. I don't want you
to get in trouble. She had many relatives living to the north. Don't
act that way with her; try to be good to her."

The Wolf had just brought in fresh meat that evening. He
went outside where the bloody meat was hanging. He found a good
piece to cut for Coyote's back and plastered it on Coyote's backbone, pressed it on firmly. Coyote felt better. He told Coyote to lay
close to the fire so the patch would warm up. Coyote said, "OK."
Wolf went hunting. Coyote lay there and talked to himself. "I'm
not supposed to do that trick to my aunt. I should have minded
my uncle. Next time I'll do what he says. I don't like my pain."

It didn't take long to heal up. Wolf said the same thing in
song to Coyote, telling him, "Go to your aunt, Coyote, go to
your aunt, and this time don't get in trouble again. She has relatives, covers a big country. This time I want you to mind me. Do
as I say. What I need now is to put her and her baby bears all to
death because she put you in bad shape. This time we'll go
around and we'll use her for our meat. This time you must mind
me. Do the same thing, pack meat, cook blood but mix it with
fine pieces of obsidian and it will cut them inside and kill them."

They prepared this. Coyote took it to Bear's camp and Wolf
went hunting. That night Coyote returned without packing those
bodies. Wolf sang, "If you put them to death you were supposed

to gather green leaves and spread them on the ground beneath the bodies so no hair or blood will touch the ground, and pack them back to the house. Dress the bodies but don't let a single hair or drop of blood on the ground or you will turn into a bear." Coyote did things right until near the end where they died of eating blood and obsidian. When he started dressing them, the hair on bear's hide kept falling on the ground. Blood kept dripping on the ground. Coyote thought it was a good way to butcher. He cut inside, the heart, lungs, and guts, and bundled them together where he had put green limbs. He just packed the meat part on his back and started home. On the way Coyote said, "I think my uncle will say I am doing my work the wrong way. He ordered that I shouldn't let the hair or blood on the ground. I'll leave this pack here and run back fast and get the other parts and put it with this load." He ran back but found nothing there but fresh footprints of many bears going to the north like Wolf had said. He followed them a ways, then stood and looked and thought of a plan. He ran back to where he had left his pack. From there the rope he had tied it with was in loops on the ground and many footprints were on the ground traveling north. He felt bad. He thought, "If I return to the house, my uncle will kill me or do something to me." But he took the rope and carried it on to the house.

Wolf was there but said nothing to Coyote. Next morning early, Wolf sang to Coyote, "My nephew, Coyote, you didn't believe me. This is the second time I asked you not to get into trouble with your aunt. We are in danger now." Coyote knew Wolf knew the mother bear and young were alive and had gone to the north.

"This time, my nephew, you must get up and make a strong rock building four stories high with a little room on top and holes on each side so I can shoot in all directions." They ate. Coyote was afraid of Wolf, so he said, "I'll try to make the building." Coyote cut trees and made a round brush building, open on one side. Coyote told Wolf, "I'm through with my house. Go see if it is good." Wolf said, "All right, I'll take a look." He said, "This is not a house. I want a strong house to stay in when enemies come."

Coyote said, "OK, I'll try again." This time Coyote built a brush shade. He came to Wolf and said, "I'm through with the house now. Come over and see it." Wolf looked and said, "This is not a fighting house. We are in danger now. Bears will come after us anytime. Get busy and build a house four rooms high." Coyote said, "OK." This time he put up a hogan, pointed at top, dirt-covered. It had a door. He told Wolf, "The house is built now. Come and look at it." Wolf said, "No." He repeated his instructions in detail, with holes at the top to shoot enemies. Coyote said, "OK," and started again. He built a rock building, put rock walls four rooms high. At the top it had four little holes on the sides, so Wolf could shoot enemies. In the evening they went to bed. Next morning Wolf said, "It looks like Mother Bear reached the north already. I had planned for you to do something else before she came back to us." So Wolf told Coyote to run out and make a line in a circle around the house and jump as far as he could and dig a hole as deep as he could so their enemies would fall off into it.

Coyote went out and jumped half the circle and they dug the hole deep. Coyote was going to be the one to fight. They stuck arrows upright in the bottom of the hole so Mother Bear would fall in and be killed and they would eat her. They fixed this hole with arrows.

The next morning it was time for Coyote to whistle through his mouth by sitting on the edge of the hole; sitting on the south of the hole facing north and be ready to jump across so Bear would jump too. Wolf would be in the building Coyote had made, with part of their food inside.

Coyote sat beside the hole. Wolf went into the top room of the tower. He looked down and told Coyote to whistle. Faced to the north, he made the wind start right away. Wind will start if you go around whistling. Wolf told him he was doing good. Later, wind started from the north, stronger and stronger. Clouds began rising, snow flying. When the snow began to hit Coyote's face he stopped whistling and asked Wolf to exchange places; the wind was too hard on his face. Wolf sang, "No, keep it up. Mother Bear and young will be coming soon. You're doing very well. Keep it up."

Mother Bear was running toward them. Coyote was afraid and wanted to run into the house. Wolf said, "Don't try to run into the house. You must face the hole and be ready to jump.

Coyote jumped across the hole and Mother Bear jumped, but Coyote was small and could turn quicker. When she jumped across, he jumped toward her, passing under her. The third time

Mother Bear missed with her hind legs and tried to pull herself up, but was too heavy and fell backwards into the hole so the arrows pierced her body. Wolf came down. He and Coyote knocked her head and killed her. They pulled her out and dressed her out, being careful of hair and blood as they were supposed to be. They hung the meat up for jerky.

Wolf cut her claws and made a belt by hanging them on a buckskin string. Then Wolf made Coyote wear it around his waist. Coyote was glad; he thought it was pretty, but Wolf said, "You can't wear it every day. Don't wear it in a crowd or for dances." They put the belt away.

They were doing good so far. A few days later Wolf worked out a plan for Coyote to start with close neighbors to tell them to put up a dance. He told Coyote to run around all four corners of the earth to tell everyone and "We'll dance with this belt. Don't tell them we have a good thing for them to see." Coyote said, "OK." The next morning Coyote went out and started to tell everyone. People began to come in and ask Wolf if he was the one putting up the dance and he said, "Yes, I have many relatives around and I want them all to have a good time." Coyote took four days to make the trip around the world. He returned and told Wolf he had told everyone. Every night people were practicing dances part of the night and sleeping the rest until Coyote returned.

Wolf asked the people to keep the dance going all night till dawn. Wolf and Coyote had a big time, quit awhile, danced awhile. They had dry meat cooked so the people could eat anytime. They kept doing it until the middle of the night.

Some of the people were dressed pretty for a round dance. Coyote saw their clothes and thought of his belt. He stopped dancing and ran to his house to look for the belt. Later he heard the dance going and didn't want to miss it so he ran back. He kept going to look for his belt. He searched off and on till daylight among the things Wolf had put away. He scraped the dirt floor all over. Finally close to the ashes he found the belt under the ground pretty well covered. He put it on and was practicing in there to the song he could hear outside. He looked at the belt on himself and thought, "It looks good. I think everyone is going to like it."

He ran to the circle and joined the dance but before he made

one round everyone looked funny, whispered to each other, and
singers lowered their voices. They had a big circle but the dancers
began to quit and prepare to go home. The circle grew smaller. By
then morning was coming, but before it was light the dancers all
stopped. All was quiet, and the people were all leaving for home.
Coyote looked around and saw this. Before sunrise everyone went
away.

Wolf said to Coyote, "Back at the house, Coyote, you find
out now. I told you not to wear this in a crowd. We are in danger
again. Right away they will return on the warpath. We must prepare to fight. Pack part of the food in the stone building. Bundle
up the scraped buckskin and pack a load of dried meat in it and
go west over the ridge and lie under the tree. Leave the camp by
itself and listen for me. If no one returns to fight, we'll separate
for four days to see if they come. If they don't come in four days
we'll say they aren't coming."

Coyote went over the ridge to wait. He heard a big noise.
The enemies fought Wolf all morning. About noon Coyote was
hungry and couldn't wait, so he prayed aloud for the enemies,
"My uncle, Wolf, is not a hard man on a fight. Try to wound
him, kill him right away. I'm hungry." Later on Coyote heard the
enemies holler. One of the men said, "Now we've got him crippled." A little later he heard another one holler and make a noise
like *boo?o.* It meant they had killed Wolf. Coyote was glad. All
was quiet before sundown for awhile. Coyote walked back and
found Wolf already dead. He had a few arrows and had some
cuts where he was dressed out. The skin was gone; just the meat
was there. He knew the enemies had taken the hide. They feared
Coyote and had left without putting Wolf in the fire. It happened
late in the fall. The first snow was when they killed Mother Bear.

By next year at the first snowfall Coyote was living there
alone and had nearly eaten everything they had. There was snow
on the ground. He thought, "I'd better go out rabbit hunting. I'll
see rabbit sign easy. This is rabbit season."

He started north that morning. He took a fast run and came
to open timber, where a lot had been burned; dead timber in the
ridges. He thought it a good place to hunt rabbits. He looked for
signs where cottontails go into holes in the timber. It is an easy
way to catch them in holes. He slowed down, and not far from
the place he saw where some people had passed by going north,

fresh tracks. It looked not far for him to catch up. He followed them and forgot about hunting rabbits.

He got up with an old lady with a burden basket, fur blanket, cane, and a little food in the basket. She moved slow. Coyote sneaked up close to see her. He circled her, running, and saw her passing. He ran to her and stopped in front of her. "Say, Old Lady, where are you going? I thought this was a cold day for an old lady to be traveling. Everyone should be inside."

The old lady was following the enemy. She didn't go fast. She was still following the enemy still this next fall. She said, "I think you are our enemy that we are afraid of." He said, "I'm just out hunting rabbits."

She hollered like ladies always holler, then said, "Once we were at a dance and Coyote used the claws of our close relative for a belt. We fought, but Coyote had disappeared. We all go to the north where he can't find us. I think you are Coyote. I smell Coyote."

Coyote said, "No, I'm not Coyote. I'm another man. Tell me what you always do in camp at night."

She said, "I think you are Coyote. You smell bad." Coyote said, "No, I'm not Coyote. They always lay around and eat up food; they don't go hunting; they are lazy. Don't fear Coyote; he's lazy."

Then Old Woman felt better. She told a story. "When my relatives got there they made camp for me. When I got there the children ran to me and said, 'Grandmother, Grandmother.' First I had danced outside the circle by myself. The second time I made a round with those kids and other relatives hanging onto me. Then I went to camp where they had wood for me, like I always do. They had Wolf's hide and had it hanging on a pole in the center."

Coyote said, "I'm glad you told me everything. You're doing all right."

Coyote was halfway mad while she told this. He knocked her down, killed her, jumped on her body, bounced up and down, and beat it with heavy wood. When he had it all mashed up, he cut it open by the hind end, picked it up and shook the body out of the skin. While it was wet he crawled inside the skin and picked up the basket and cane and imitated her gait.

By the time he reached camp, he saw a big round dance at one end, but still he walked slow. Children ran out and hung on his clothes. He danced around outside of the circle, one round. He saw a short guy, a badger, on one side and a porcupine opposite. On the second round when he came to the short man he jumped over, grabbed his hide, jumped across, and ran off.

People said, "That was our enemy." They started chasing him south. Good runners at first nearly caught up with him but just before they could grab him he figured to turn into something. he made a sharp turn and turned into a dead cedar tree nearly rotted down. They passed by and didn't see him ahead, so they returned, circled around, found his tracks, and came toward him. He turned into a human again. They saw Coyote ahead and almost overtook him again. He made a turn behind a tree and turned into a jumping cactus [the cholla cactus, *Opuntia bigelovii*]. They passed by him. He watched them go around, return, and track him. Coyote turned into a man again and ran. They saw him and ran after him again. He started whistling again, trying to make the wind blow. Coyote saw nuts from the oak brush. They were round with holes in, like fruit. The dried shells were empty. Worms grew inside. Coyote went inside that hole. The nuts were rolling by him. They were lightweight. He said, "This is the thing I'm asking. He jumped inside and the wind rolled it on south slowly, but Coyote thought no one would find him. He thought he was far enough so he came out and looked around and went on to his camp.

He didn't think his enemies would come that far after him. He stayed there the next day. In the morning he thought of a way to try to make Wolf come alive. Coyote put a skin down where he had a pile of old wolf bones. He put all the bones inside the skin. He put it over his feet and kicked it. The bones and hide were dry. He kicked it west, with no result. He kicked it south. Each time he returned to the same place. There was no result. He tried again toward the east. It felt like the bones were heavy when it started out and it was a wolf when it lit on its feet. He wiped his face and exhaled twice. Wolf said, "What's wrong with me. I have been asleep here hard."

Coyote said, "Yes, I've had a tough time here. You weren't asleep." He told him what happened.

Wolf said, "I was asleep all this time. I wasn't dead." He told Coyote to start a fire and cook food. Before they had a lot of food, but now they had none. Wolf said, "I'm going out of here and hunt for food." He started the next morning, killed a deer, packed it in, and roasted it different ways, like in former times.

They stayed there awhile. While Wolf was dead all that time, his spirit had left the bones. His spirit had gone underground and found a lady for his wife. He stayed with her until Coyote put the skin and bones together.

Wolf thought of the lady while hunting but said nothing to Coyote. Then Wolf told Coyote to cook meat well done for the next meal. He put a pot on the fire. Coyote went to gather wood to keep his fire going and the pot boiling. Coyote kept doing this, with more and more wood each time. Later in the day, Wolf decided the boiling pot on the fire would be a good way to jump in and go underground and get the lady he had left. He did it while Coyote was outside. Wolf went through the pot, underground to the lady. He thought Coyote would never come to where he was, but when Coyote returned, he missed Wolf and looked all around the fire, and saw no sign of Wolf leaving, just footprints by the fire. Later on Coyote thought, "I think this is the place where my Uncle Wolf went in. I don't want to stay here alone." He tried to jump in but each time he was afraid and drew back. Finally he got up courage and jumped in. Then he saw wolf footprints and tracked him to the home where Wolf and his wife lived. Wolf said, "Coyote, you have come to my place. I have a place to stay, but I'm glad you've come." Wolf had a pretty young lady for his wife. All three stayed together.

Wolf and his wife slept on one side of the fire. Coyote stayed on the other side. Coyote kept wood on the fire, so there was light, and he watched every night to see what Wolf was doing with his wife. Later Wolf asked Coyote to go out on the ridge. Wolf said, "I saw some long timbers over the ridge. Go over, break off branches and pack them. Bring the tree trunk to burn on the fire."

Coyote said, "I believe I see a mountain sheep over here, my uncle. Come along. Shoot at them. There are big ones lying under an overhanging wall. I lay out over the wall and looked underneath."

Wolf said, "OK," so both went to the place. Coyote had put the heads of dead mountain sheep in a line under the wall, bedded down. Wolf went slow and said, "Where are sheep bedded around here?" Coyote said, "Lean over and look." Wolf looked and drew back, then looked again. Coyote pushed him off the high wall. Coyote wanted him to be killed. Coyote ran back to the camp to Wolf's wife and tried to grab her for his wife, but she was scared and pushed him away. Coyote kept touching her and tried to get her, but she kept fighting. She kept jumping in one spot and she sunk into the ground which was like quicksand.

By then Wolf had climbed the wall and came to camp. He said nothing. He knew Coyote must have fooled with his wife. That was the reason she was gone.

Later on Coyote said, "We'd better go back up above. We'll have better light and a better time." Wolf agreed. So they went back. By then the wind was getting stronger, later in the year. Wolf told Coyote to go over to the ridge and get wood for the fire. "We may have snow on the ground before morning." Wind from the south usually makes snow.

Coyote said, "OK," picked a long tree, and packed it back on his shoulder to the house. The wind was strong; it came in gusts bringing snow. It was hard to see ahead. Coyote came with the wood. He called, "My uncle, Wolf, I am bringing long wood for the fire. I might hit you. Holler if I get too close." Wolf heard him coming. He reached to one side, got a cane, dug it under hot ashes, and blew two hard breaths toward the east. He told Coyote not to come to the fire. "Pass by and go to the east. By giving me trouble, I'll give you a chance to turn into a star. Climb up to the sky and come in the sky this time of year. When dawn is coming Coyote's star is rising in the east. You'll be a big star, turn on the cold, sometimes bring snow and cold weather; a big star with a big log (four stars) in a bow above it.

Wolf stayed at that camp. He wished for his wife underground.

Wolf, Coyote, Bat, and Elk

When animals were human, two persons, Wolf and Coyote, always stayed with big animals. They had someone to cook for them. They lived toward the west on the edge of a big ocean where many people lived. They had many games and had lots of fun, but Wolf found out no big animals were living there. They just had small ones, Cottontail and Jackrabbit. Wolf used them for meat. After he killed them he couldn't make moccasins with their sinew. He always was mending his moccasins. One evening Wolf asked Coyote to use what they had, bedding and clothing. Next day Coyote was having a lot of fun betting these things on games, betting rugs, feathers, for arrows, and other things. Wolf told him to bet them, and after he lost everything in four days, Wolf planned to make a trip to Pine [Walapai] Mountain just south of Kingman. So Coyote gambled, had fun, and lost many things until all was gone. In four days and nights, Coyote asked Wolf to move toward the east in the morning. Wolf did not count by days; his way was to call each year a day. Coyote thought he meant four days. After four years Coyote and Wolf started east. They traveled along. When the sun was getting low, Wolf saw jackrabbits jump up and run along. Wolf began to whistle at the jackrabbits, and they were witched by Wolf's whistle. Coyote ran to the dead rabbits and picked up five or six. The load was heavy for Coyote to pack. They stopped early to camp out, gathered small sticks, dug a hole, and built a fire mixed with rocks to heat the rocks. When the rocks were red hot, they skinned the rabbits, took the insides out and put it away, and lay them at the foot of a brush enclosure they had made for camp. Wolf told Coyote not to bother the insides when they traveled on the next day. They barbequed the rabbits; put them in the fire and covered them with dirt. They roasted till morning, when they uncovered them and were ready to eat. Wolf told Coyote not to eat bones, to eat only meat, but leave a little meat and pile it with the inside part. Wolf said, "By doing this we'll be safe on our journey, but if you happen to eat the insides or all the meat from the bone, then rabbits will keep on running and I won't be able to witch them with my whistle and we'll starve before we reach Pine Mountain." They hunted this way and did the same thing each day until they were halfway on their journey. Coyote began to think of the bones and the little meat and thought, "Why do we leave them at our camp each time?" Coyote was getting hungry before evening when Wolf got the rabbits. So, just before they reached Pine Mountain, Coyote hid out and made believe he was almost to make his toilet. He said, "I need to go to the toilet." Wolf said, "OK, but don't take too long." Coyote said, "OK," and ran back to where the inside meat and bones had been left that morning. He ate it all, filled up, and felt better. He overtook Wolf and said he was feeling better.

Toward evening Wolf began to whistle but the jackrabbit went on
its way, shook his long ears, and ran fast and disappeared. Wolf
knew what Coyote had done that morning. The next rabbit the
Wolf whistled to again, but the rabbit kept on going. That night
they had nothing to eat. Wolf said nothing to Coyote but the next
morning he said, "You didn't listen to me. If you want it that way
we'll camp out hungry. If you had minded me we would have rabbits. Now we have none from here on." So they camped out hungry without food from there to Pine Mountain.

Wolf knew that a natural water hole had big animals living
under the water and that was where Wolf had wished to go. Wolf
told Coyote to dive under the water and catch an elk by its horns
and bring him up to the top. "If you bring it up, water will
bubble and rise up. If you bring him up in the middle of the day
he'll be wet; he'll roll around near the water hole and after his hair
dries the elk will get up and start walking east. Elk is not a dryland
animal. He lives under the water here, and he will travel east to
the big ocean. So I want to kill him when he gets up from the sand
and walks a little way. So, we can sneak up before he starts running. We can use his hide for our home and can dry sinew to sew
our moccasins. It will be as long as our two arms. This is the kind
of animal I wish to kill." Coyote said, "OK, OK, my uncle. Uncle,
I'll jump in that water hole tomorrow morning." Next morning
Wolf told Coyote to jump in. Coyote pretended to jump in but
drew back and teased Wolf until Wolf was halfway sore at him.
Wolf told Coyote to watch the water hole and he would dive in
himself. He told Coyote not to shoot the water. "It will boil up
when I am on my way down and when you see the elk coming up
I'll be on my way down. When you see the elk coming up, I'll be
on his horns, so don't shoot then. But after he gets through rolling
around, shoot at his belly from behind and you might hit his heart.
But don't shoot the water while I am there."

The sun was halfway up and Wolf dived in. The water began
to rise up and boil, so Coyote thought the elk was on his way up.
Coyote got his arrows and began to shoot in the water one by one
until all the arrows were wasted. Then Coyote sat and watched the
water. After awhile he saw Elk's head come up. It was huge, with
big horns. Elk climbed up on a bluff, rolled around, shook his hair,
and finally all dried up. Wolf was in the elk's horns, lying there.
He saw Coyote standing nearby without arrows.

Coyote asked Wolf to hang onto a limb as the elk passed close to some trees on its way. Elk started to walk, then began to trot, walk, and trot. Coyote said, "There's a tree. Grab the tree and make the elk stop." Wolf said, "No, I won't. You want me to go to the big ocean. Elk won't stop at a mountain, timber, or anyplace. He is thinking of a big ocean where he wants to go. You are the one who is supposed to shoot him, but you used up your arrows. Just never mind."

The elk went along to Walapai Mountain, on east to Floyd Mountain, Bill Williams Mountain, to the San Francisco Peaks, across the open desert, and finally came to a place where he could almost see the big ocean waves. He saw one more mountain ahead, south of Pica. Wolf knew all the way that from that mountain he would run and could jump two draws together when running. After Elk passed the San Francisco Peaks he would run as fast as a horse, then he would slow down, tired out. He knew there was the camp of a family, Bat, with many kids, close to the ocean. The children saw Elk approaching. They heard songs of Wolf as he called to Bat, "My grandfather, I'm bringing you a big animal to kill." The children went inside and told Bat come look at what was coming.

Bat told his wife to lie on the ground and he tied one leg of his wife to one side of the house and the other leg to the other side of the house. Bat was having intercourse with his wife. He wiped his penis with buckskin and put it by his head and said it would cause a headache. Next it would cause cold, body ache, diarrhea, and illness to cause death. He tied them, the diseases, up in a robe and put them away. But Father Bat told his children not to bother him when they kept coming. "I'm doing something." The elk passed by, and the bat saw it. He thought it was a good animal to kill, so Bat quit what he was doing and got his bow. He put it against the wall, without a string, and got grass to use for food. He blew and spit on the grass and rolled it into string and made a string for the bow. The only stick he had was a fire drill stick, no arrow. He took charcoal and blackened the end and made it for a point. He wrapped it with string. He had no feather. Elk was tired and hadn't gone far. Bat went toward Elk. Wolf called out, "Run close and shoot under his belly before he goes under the ocean." Bat shot. Elk trotted a little ways and fell dead at the edge where waves washed up over part of his body.

From there the elk increased in the ocean and the horns were different. They were flat.

Bat's family brought a blanket and wrapped the elk in it. They skinned and cut up the meat. They packed it a little at a time to camp. They started boiling meat for Wolf. He was bony and almost starved. Bat gave him some of the meat to eat, but the meat went through his body and passed through right away. He couldn't hold it like we eat and just go to the toilet once in awhile. He had a hole where the food went out.

Bat thought it over and decided what would be a good plan to fix Wolf's hind. Bat got a piece from inside Elk's body and put it on Wolf's hind and plastered it against the bone part, and left a little hole, and made it part of Wolf's hide. So later he could hold his food and when pain comes on his body he knows he needs to go to the toilet. Then the food did some good and Wolf built up again and felt good. Then he told Bat he wanted to run to the camp where he had lived before. Bat said he thought it was time for him to go back. So, the next morning Bat gave him some meat to take back.

In the first day he reached Coyote at Pine Mountain. He reached it that evening. Before he went to camp he hung up his pack and went slow to listen if Coyote was still alive. He heard no sound. He stood in front of Coyote, but Coyote was almost starved to death. Coyote listened for Wolf. He thought Wolf still alive and Wolf might come anytime.

A fly was buzzing near Coyote's ear. He snapped at it to eat but it flew out of reach. Coyote said, "I want to listen for my uncle, Wolf." Coyote had his eyes shut and didn't see Wolf standing there. Wolf spoke and said, "Coyote what are you saying? I'm hungry, starving. What are we going to eat?" Coyote said, "I used up the last cornmeal we had this morning." Wolf said, "What are we going to eat this evening?" Coyote said, "Nothing here." Wolf said, "I pack a little piece of meat here. You have to pack it here." Coyote said, "Yes, I'll do it." He got up and started running to get it, glad that he was going to get food. He found a big pile of meat. He didn't want to wait, so he started to eat, and filled up. So Coyote started to pack the meat but couldn't lift it all. Coyote ran back to Wolf and told him it was too heavy. Wolf went and threw it over his shoulder and said, "It's nothing to me." He packed it to camp and they ate it, but had no hide.

They stayed in the same camp that fall. Wolf figured out a way that Coyote shouldn't stay with him any longer. One evening he said, "It's late in the evening. It's windy. Will you fetch a big long log?" Coyote was scared of Wolf and said, "OK." He went to hunt a log to put on the fire till morning. He found one and packed it on his back. Wolf put a cane under hot ashes and told Coyote not to return to camp. Wolf blew on his hands and expelled his breath. "Coyote, just miss our camp and keep going east packing that wood. When you come to the sky, go up on it and turn into a Coyote-Packing-Wood star.

Coyote kept on going and did as Wolf said he should. He went up on the sky and turned into a star, the Wood-Packer star. By almost morning he climbed up in the sky. He kept saying to Wolf, "If I let this log fall down it might hit you." It is a big star with four smaller ones in an arch above it, Coyote with a pack.

The First Sweatlodge

Coyote built the first sweatlodge alone. Wolf told him how to do it, and Coyote did the work. Wolf stayed around and told him and watched him build it. Wolf told Coyote to cut mesquite wood to make fire to heat rocks. "Don't use just any kind of rock and don't use red sandstone [it spalls explosively when heated]. Get hard, white rock [limestone]. Use any kind of wood to build the sweatlodge. Make it big enough for two people. Use any number of supporting sticks, then wrap others around and tie them in place. Don't cover it with dirt." Wolf got a buffalo hide and put it all over the top. (In another version, the sweatlodge frame was covered with a rabbit fur robe.)

Coyote began the sweatlodge in the morning and finished it about noon. Coyote built a fire and heated some rocks for about an hour; the rocks got hot quickly.

Wolf went inside and stayed in. He put water on the rocks and made steam. He sang to himself two or three times and lay in there about an hour to think. Coyote reached his hand inside the buffalo hide and kept putting water on the rock to make steam. Wolf lay in there till nearly sundown and Coyote stayed around outside. He sat on the ground by the door and wouldn't let Wolf out. Wolf got "all in" and just lay down. Then Coyote took him out and thought Wolf was pretty near dead. He lifted the buffalo skin up, pulled Wolf out by the arm, and dragged him about forty or fifty feet. Then he got a wildcat hide blanket, covered him up, and left him there all night. When dawn came, Wolf woke up. He felt good and strong, so he went hunting deer.

Coyote and Deer

(A children's story.)

Coyote went to the place where Deer lived alone. Coyote saw Deer, and they sat together and talked, told stories. They were glad to see one another. This deer had a bow and arrows. Deer asked Coyote to stay quiet. Deer took his bow and arrows a short distance away and shot an arrow into the air. He knew where it would hit. Deer watched it fall, and ran to where it would land. He turned his backside so it entered his (anus). Then he withdrew it with fat from his inside. They cooked it and ate it. When Coyote was ready to leave, he asked Deer how he had done it. He thought it was an animal Deer had killed. Coyote said, "I'm glad you told me that. You come to my camp in four days and we'll eat together the same way."

Coyote went home, took his bow and arrows, and tried it himself. But the arrow entered his (anus) and killed him. When Deer came by four day later, he found Coyote dead.

Coyote's Death

(A children's story.)

Beetle has a hard shell. He pretends to be dead if touched. But he can fly.

Beetle was hungry and wished for food. He put a hard cover over his back so nothing could hurt his body. He lay on the trail where sheep passed by to water. He waited on a ledge where sheep came. Some sheep came by. The first one stepped on Beetle and slipped and fell. He lay there moaning. One after another did this and broke their legs. Then Beetle arose and killed all of the mountain sheep. He skinned them and took the meat to where he lived. He put the meat up to dry on poles. Coyote thought he would call on Beetle and see how he was. He saw much meat and said, "I'm kind of low on food so I thought I would visit you." They talked for awhile, then Beetle got some meat and boiled it for Coyote to eat before he went. He gathered a big bunch of meat and fat together for Coyote to take home. When the boiled meat was done, they ate together. After eating Coyote asked how to kill it without a bow and arrow. So Beetle told Coyote all about it.

Coyote said, "OK, I know your story. Four days from now you must visit me. I'll hunt your way, and we'll have meat and eat together."

Four days later Beetle visited Coyote's camp. He waited several days for Coyote to return. Beetle tracked Coyote and found the place where mountain sheep had a trail to water. He found Coyote already dead. Mountain sheep had passed by, stepped on him, and had mashed him to pieces.

Bibliography

Anonymous
    1899   The Yava-Supai Indian. *Arizona Graphic*, Vol. 14, Oct. 7.
Curtis, Edward S.
    1908   *The North American Indian*, Vol. 2. The University Press, Cambridge.
Cushing, F. H.
    1882   The Nation of the Willows, Pts. 1 and 2. *Atlantic Monthly*, Vol. 50, No. 299, pp. 362–74; No. 100, pp. 541–59.
Dobyns, Henry F., and Robert C. Euler
    1960   A Brief History of the Northeastern Pai. *Plateau*, Vol. 32, No. 3, pp. 49–57.
Dobyns, Henry F., and Robert C. Euler, Eds.
    1961   The Origins of the Pai Tribes, by Henry P. Ewing. *Kiva*, Vol. 26, No. 3.
Euler, Robert C. , and Henry F. Dobyns, Eds.
    1960   The Pai Tribes, by Henry P. Ewing. *Ethnohistory*, Vol. 7, No. 1, pp. 61–80.
Iliff, Flora G.
    1954   *People of the Blue Water*. Harper and Brothers, New York.
James, George W.
    1903   *Indians of the Painted Desert Region*. Little, Brown and Co., Boston.
    1907   *In and Around the Grand Canyon*. Little, Brown and Co., Boston.
Kroeber, A. L., Ed.
    1935   Walapai Ethnography. *American Anthropological Association, Memoirs*, No. 42.
Smithson, Carma Lee
    1959   The Havasupai Woman. *University of Utah Anthropological Papers*, No. 38.
Spier, Leslie
    1928   Havasupai Ethnography. *American Museum of Natural History, Anthropological Papers*, No. 29, pp. 81–392.
    1929   Problems Arising from the Cultural Position of the Havasupai. *American Anthropologist*, Vol. 31, No. 2, pp. 213–22.
Whiting, Alfred F.
    ca.   *Havasupai Habitat*. Unpublished MS, Museum of Northern Arizona, Flagstaff.
    1941